The Standard for English Grammar Books

GRAMMAR ZONE
WORKBOOK

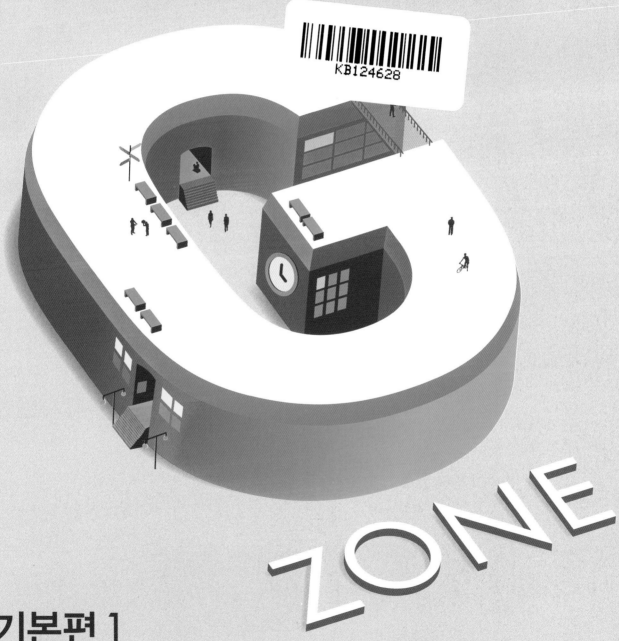

KB124628

ZONE

기본편 1

GRAMMAR ZONE
WORKBOOK 기본편 1

지은이	NE능률 영어교육연구소
선임연구원	한정은
연구원	배연희 이하나 송민아 이경란 강혜진
영문교열	Patrick Ferraro Benjamin Robinson
표지 · 내지디자인	닷츠
맥편집	허문희
영업	한기영 이경구 박인규 정철교 김남준 이우현
마케팅	박혜선 남경진 이지원 김여진

Let's grow together

NE능률이
미래를
창조합니다.

건강한 배움의 고객가치를 제공하겠다는 꿈을 실현하기 위해
40년이 넘는 시간 동안 열심히 달려왔습니다.

앞으로도 끊임없는 연구와 노력을 통해
당연한 것을 멈추지 않고

고객, 기업, 직원 모두가 함께 성장하는 NE능률이 되겠습니다.

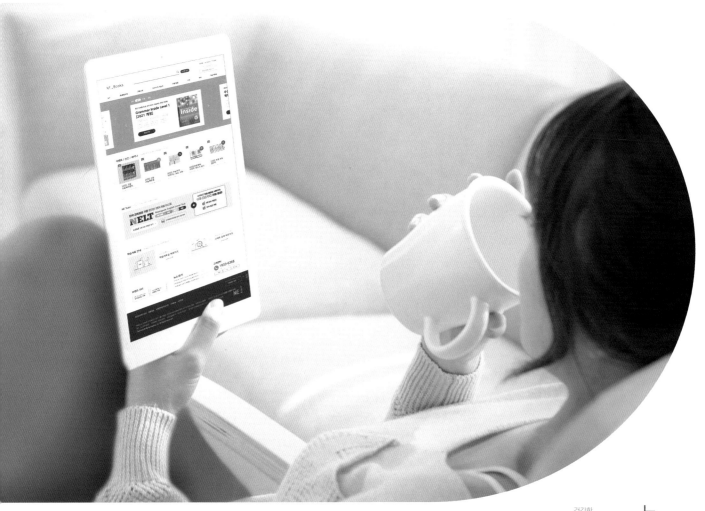

Practice is the best of all instructions.

연습은 가장 좋은 가르침이다.

———

유명한 운동 선수, 최고의 과학자, 노벨상을 받은 작가, 그 누구도 자신들이 이루어낸 것이 하루 아침에 완성되었다고 말하는 사람은 없습니다. 그들을 성공으로 이끈 것은 무엇일까요? 여러분도 알다시피 목표를 달성하고 꿈을 이루는 데 성실하게 연습하는 것만큼 효과적인 무기는 없습니다. 저희는 여러분을 '문법 지존(至尊)'의 세계로 인도할 수 있는 가장 좋은 무기를 준비하였습니다. G-ZONE에서 학습한 모든 것을 이 WORKBOOK을 통해 연습하여 여러분 모두 문법의 '지존'이 되길 바랍니다. 꾸준한 연습을 다짐하는 여러분을 응원합니다.

구성과 특징

진단 TEST

현재 자신이 알고 있는 문법 항목과 모르는 문법 항목을 점검할 수 있게 하는 TEST입니다. WORKBOOK을 본격적으로 공부하기 전에 진단 TEST부터 풀어 보고, 자신이 부족한 부분이 어디인지 파악한 후 학습 계획을 세워 봅시다. 각 문제 옆에는 연관된 Grammar Zone 본 교재의 UNIT이 표기되어 있으니, 틀린 문제에 해당하는 UNIT을 본 교재로 먼저 복습하면 효율적인 학습이 가능합니다.

TEST

각 UNIT을 제대로 학습하였는지 확인할 수 있는 다양한 유형의 문제를 수록하였습니다. 비교적 간단한 드릴형 문제에서부터 사고력과 응용력을 요하는 문제까지 꼼꼼히 풀어본 후 부족한 부분에 대해 추가 학습 계획을 세워 봅시다.

CHECK UP •

각 UNIT의 핵심 문법을 간단한 문제를 통해 확인할 수 있습니다. 각 문제 옆에는 해당 문법을 다룬 본 교재의 항목이 표시되어 있으므로, 추가 학습이 필요하다면 해당 항목을 복습한 후 WORKBOOK으로 돌아오세요.

WRITING PRACTICE

쓰기 연습이 가능한 문제를 충분히 제시하였습니다. 수행평가나 서술형 문제 대비가 가능하며 궁극적으로 영어 쓰기 실력을 향상시켜 줍니다.

실전 TEST & 최종 TEST

여러 CHAPTER의 문법 사항을 종합적으로 확인할 수 있도록 총 6회의 실전 TEST와 4회의 최종 TEST를 제공합니다. 중간고사 및 기말고사에 대비할 수 있도록 문제 유형과 난이도 등을 실제에 맞추어 구성하였으며, 실제 기출을 응용한 주관식 문제를 제시하여 수행평가 및 서술형 문제 대비에도 유용합니다.

Contents

Study Tracker

그래머존 본책의 학습일을 기입한 후, 워크북으로 확인 학습한 날짜도 함께 적어 봅시다. 워크북까지 학습을 끝낸 후 '나의 문법 이해도'를 점검해 봅시다.

본책 CHAPTER / 학습일			워크북 TEST / 학습일									나의 문법 이해도		
			진단 TEST						월		일	상	중	하
CHAPTER 01 시제	월	일	01 월 일			02 월 일			03 월 일			상	중	하
			04 월 일			05 월 일			06 월 일					
			07 월 일			08 월 일								
CHAPTER 02 조동사	월	일	09 월 일			10 월 일			11 월 일			상	중	하
			12 월 일			13 월 일			14 월 일					
CHAPTER 03 수동태	월	일	15 월 일			16 월 일			17 월 일			상	중	하
			18 월 일											
			실전 TEST 01						월		일	상	중	하
CHAPTER 04 부정사	월	일	19 월 일			20 월 일			21 월 일			상	중	하
			22 월 일			23 월 일			24 월 일					
			25 월 일			26 월 일								
CHAPTER 05 동명사	월	일	27 월 일			28 월 일			29 월 일			상	중	하
			30 월 일											
			실전 TEST 02						월		일	상	중	하
CHAPTER 06 분사	월	일	31 월 일			32 월 일			33 월 일			상	중	하
			34 월 일											
CHAPTER 07 접속사와 절	월	일	35 월 일			36 월 일			37 월 일			상	중	하
			38 월 일											
			실전 TEST 03						월		일	상	중	하
			최종 TEST 01						월		일	상	중	하
			최종 TEST 02						월		일	상	중	하

진단 TEST

UNIT 1 1 A vegetarian is a person who _____ meat or fish.
① eat never   ② eats never   ③ never eat   ④ never eats

UNIT 1 2 I'll email you as soon as I _____ home from work.
① get   ② got   ③ will get   ④ am getting

★ **UNIT 1,2,3** 3 Our flight _____ at Jeju airport at 2 p.m.
① arrives   ② is arriving   ③ will arrive   ④ has arrived

UNIT 2 4 A: Tom, someone is at the door. Can you get it?   B: Okay. _____.
① I will   ② I'm going to   ③ I am   ④ I do

★ **UNIT 4** 5 I _____ that Admiral Yi Sunshin was one of Korea's greatest heroes.
① think   ② am thinking   ③ thought   ④ have thought

UNIT 6 6 A: Is she married?   B: Yes, she _____ for 3 years.
① marries   ② married   ③ is married   ④ has been married

UNIT 6 7 His son _____ church. He's not at home now.
① has gone to   ② has gone for   ③ has been to   ④ has been for

★ **UNIT 7** 8 _____ read the *Harry Potter* series?
① Did you   ② Have you   ③ When did you   ④ When have you

UNIT 9 9 If you try your best, you _____ get into medical school.
① will can   ② will be able to   ③ will be going to   ④ can will

★ **UNIT 11** 10 _____ join our baseball team?
① Would you   ② Shall you   ③ Will you   ④ Would you like to

UNIT 12 11 I _____ over to change a flat tire. It took a long time.
① had to pull   ② should have pulled ③ ought not to   ④ must pull

UNIT 12 12 Many witnesses insisted that the fire _____ in a trash can.
① should start   ② start   ③ has started   ④ had started

UNIT 14 13 She _____ angry yesterday, because she left without saying a word.
① must be   ② must have been   ③ should be   ④ should have been

UNIT 15 14 The man _____ after he left a box on the table.
① disappear   ② disappeared   ③ is disappeared   ④ was disappeared

UNIT 18 15 He is well known _____ his books about dinosaurs.
① by   ② to   ③ as   ④ for

UNIT 19	**16**	They agreed _____ or use any products from the company.

① to don't buy   ② to buy not   ③ not to buy   ④ not buy

★ | UNIT 20 | **17** | They _____ to boost exports. |

① want   ② expect   ③ need   ④ encourage

★ | UNIT 22 | **18** | He dyed his hair _____ younger than he really is. |

① to look   ② in order to look   ③ so as to look   ④ for looking

| UNIT 24 | **19** | It was stupid _____ to trust strangers in a foreign country. |

① of him   ② of his   ③ for him   ④ for his

| UNIT 25 | **20** | He had his car _____ yesterday. |

① wash   ② washed   ③ to wash   ④ washing

| UNIT 26 | **21** | First-class passengers _____ carry two pieces of baggage. |

① allow   ② allow to   ③ are allowed   ④ are allowed to

| UNIT 29 | **22** | Here are some tips to avoid _____ a victim of terrorism. |

① becoming   ② to become   ③ to becoming   ④ become

| UNIT 29 | **23** | I'm very busy now, so please stop _____ me. |

① bother   ② to bother   ③ bothering   ④ bothers

★ | UNIT 30 | **24** | I'm really looking forward to _____. |

① it   ② the movie   ③ see the movie   ④ seeing the movie

| UNIT 31 | **25** | Who is the girl _____ sunglasses in this picture? |

① wearing   ② to wear   ③ worn   ④ wear

| UNIT 32 | **26** | I lost my appetite, so I left the food _____. |

① untouch   ② untouched   ③ untouching   ④ to untouch

| UNIT 34 | **27** | She fell asleep with the computer _____. |

① turn on   ② turning on   ③ turned on   ④ to turn on

| UNIT 35 | **28** | Stay away from junk food, _____ you'll be out of shape. |

① and   ② or   ③ but   ④ so

| UNIT 1, 36 | **29** | I wonder if my dad _____ me to use his car. |

① allow   ② allows   ③ will allow   ④ allowed

| UNIT 38 | **30** | It was _____ a perfect day that I couldn't just stay at home. |

① so   ② such   ③ much   ④ very

↗ **CHECK UP**   괄호 안에서 알맞은 것을 고르시오.

1 The students will be happy when school (will be / is) over.   `B-2`

2 Nowadays Tim (goes / went) to piano practice on Thursdays.   `A-2`

3 Giraffes (live / lived) in Africa.   `A-4`

4 I doubt if Jim (will pass / passes) the test.   `B-2`

5 A human first (walks / walked) on the Moon in 1969.   `C`

A   괄호 안에 주어진 말을 현재시제 또는 과거시제로 바꾸어 빈칸에 쓰시오.

1 I was feeling tired, so I _____ for an hour. (sleep)

2 I'll be waiting at the bus station until Sara _____. (arrive)

3 The show was boring, so I _____ for long. (not / stay)

4 How _____ you _____ the situation last year? (handle)

5 It always _____ when I go camping. (rain)

6 The last time I went to the airport, I _____ my passport. (lose)

B   보기에 주어진 말을 알맞은 형태로 바꾸어 빈칸에 쓰시오.

보기	eat	go	study	come back	write	hurry

1 Trevor never _____ Chinese food. He hates it.

2 Shakespeare _____ many famous plays.

3 Jimmy _____ on vacation twice last year.

4 A : How did you learn to speak French?

    B : I _____ it on the Internet.

5 Can I ask when you _____?

6 If we _____, we'll catch the bus.

C 다음 문장에서 어법상 <u>틀린</u> 곳을 찾아 고치시오. 틀린 곳이 없으면 O표 하시오.

1 In 1901, Queen Victoria, head of the British Empire, died.

2 Columbus live during the 18th century.

3 People all over the world ate Asian food nowadays.

4 The White House was located in Washington D.C.

5 She will pick me up as soon as she will finish the work.

D 자연스러운 대화가 되도록 괄호 안에서 알맞은 것을 고르시오.

1 A : When (do / did) you last see Mike?

   B : I (see / saw) him last Saturday.

2 A : What are you going to do after you (graduate / will graduate)?

   B : I'm thinking of doing an internship.

3 A : What do you do on weekends?

   B : I usually (play / played) video games at home.

WRITING PRACTICE

괄호 안의 말을 이용하여 영작을 완성하시오.

1 다음 열차는 5분 후에 올 것입니다. (next train, come)

   The _____ _____ _____ in five minutes.

2 나는 그가 오자마자 그에게 그 이야기를 해 줄 것이다. (tell, arrive)

   I _____ _____ him the story as soon as he _____.

3 날씨가 따뜻해서 나는 코트를 벗었다. (warm, take off)

   It _____ _____, so I _____ _____ my coat.

4 그 배우는 작년에 아카데미 상을 받았다. (receive, an Academy Award)

   The actor _____ _____ _____ _____ last year.

5 너는 보통 몇 시에 일어나니? (usually, wake up)

   What time _____ _____ _____ _____ _____?

UNIT 02 미래시제

A-2
A-3
B-2
A-2

☑ CHECK UP   괄호 안에서 알맞은 것을 고르시오.

1 A: I've got to go to the dentist tomorrow.

B: I (will / am going to) give you a ride if you like.

2 A: Why are you carrying a paintbrush?

B: I (will / am going to) paint my bedroom.

3 We (go / are going) shopping. Would you like to come along?

4 Oh, the door is open. I (will / am going to) go and shut it.

A

괄호 안에 주어진 말과 will 또는 be going to을 이용하여 빈칸을 완성하시오.

1 Look at those kids! They _____ an accident. (have)

2 Don't worry about the trash. I _____ it out now. (take)

3 She is pregnant, and she _____ a baby in June. (have)

4 Jane can't meet us tomorrow, as she _____ her driving test. (take)

5 I _____ for lunch if you pay for dinner tonight. (pay)

B

보기에 주어진 말과 will 또는 be going to을 이용하여 빈칸을 완성하시오.

보기	do	watch	forget	have	be late

1 A : Do you want to play cards?

B : No, I _____ a documentary on TV.

2 A : I don't want to pick up the groceries today.

B : Okay. I _____ it.

3 It's nearly eight now. We _____.

4 A : You forgot to wash the dishes again.

B : I'm sorry. I promise I _____ (not) again.

5 I _____ the number three combo, please.

C 밑줄 친 부분의 의미로 알맞은 것을 연결하시오.

1 We're stuck in traffic. It is going to be a long trip home. •   • a. future plan

2 I'm taking five courses next semester. •   • b. making a promise

3 If I get another chance, I won't let you down again. •   • c. making a prediction

D 자연스러운 대화가 되도록 괄호 안에서 알맞은 것을 고르시오.

1 A : What are you going to do during summer vacation?

B : I (learn / am going to learn) Chinese.

2 A : That box looks heavy. I (am going to / will) help you with it.

B : Thank you.

3 A : Is this your snowboard? (Are you going to / Will you) start snowboarding?

B : Yes. My first lesson is next week!

WRITING PRACTICE

보기에 주어진 말을 이용하여 영작을 완성하시오.

보기	post	turn off	rain	play	come

1 그는 다음 달에 경기에서 뛸 것이다.

He _____ _____ _____ _____ in the game next month.

2 저기 우체통이 있다. 이 편지들을 부쳐야겠다.

There is a mailbox over there. I _____ _____ _____ _____.

3 A: 수돗물을 틀어놨구나. B: 죄송해요. 잠글게요.

A: You've left the water on.
B: I'm sorry. I _____ _____ _____ _____.

4 그 밴드는 콘서트를 위해 한국에 올 것이다.

The band _____ _____ _____ _____ to Korea for a concert.

5 저 먹구름 좀 봐. 비가 오겠다.

Look at those black clouds. It _____ _____ _____ _____.

UNIT 03 진행형

정답 및 해설 p.06

☑ **CHECK UP** **괄호 안에서 알맞은 것을 고르시오.**

1 Please don't make so much noise. I (try / am trying) to sleep. `A-1`

2 Don't call our house after ten tonight. The baby (sleeps / will be sleeping). `C`

3 Joan was working out when I (stopped / am stopping) by her house. `B-2`

4 A: You (will be working / are working) hard today! `A-2`

　　B: Yes, I have lots of work.

A　**괄호 안에 주어진 말을 현재진행형, 과거진행형 또는 미래진행형으로 바꾸어 빈칸에 쓰시오.**

1 This time next year, I _____ university. (attend)

2 Alex _____ computer games when we arrived. (play)

3 I'm really busy now. I _____ my father paint the house. (help)

4 By the time I get home, my husband _____ dinner. (make)

B　**주어진 말을 순서대로 활용하여 과거시제와 과거진행형을 이용한 문장을 만드시오.**

0 my friend / call / while / I / eat lunch

　　→ My friend called while I was eating lunch.

1 while / I / shop / I / meet / Mandy

　　→ _____

2 he / come / home / while / I / wash / the dishes

　　→ _____

3 while / I / walk down / the road / I / see / Bill

　　→ _____

4 Jim / argue with / his mother / when / I / call / him

　　→ _____

5 I / burn / my finger / when / I / make / spaghetti

→ _____

6 when / I / visit Sarah / she / make / her bed

→ _____

C 자연스러운 대화가 되도록 괄호 안에서 알맞은 것을 고르시오.

1 A : Mike, can you take out the trash for me?

B : Can I do it later? I (watch / am watching) my favorite TV show now.

2 A : Why didn't you answer my call last night?

B : Sorry, I (was preparing / will be preparing) dinner.

3 A : Tim's such a whiner.

B : Yes, he (is always complaining / was always complaining) about something.

WRITING PRACTICE

괄호 안의 말과 진행형을 이용하여 영작을 완성하시오.

1 엄마는 항상 내게 숙제를 끝마치기 전에는 TV를 보지 말라고 말씀하신다. (always, tell, me)

My mom _____ _____ _____ _____ not to watch TV
before finishing my homework.

2 Kate가 도착했을 때, 우리는 야구 경기를 보고 있었다. (arrive, watch)

_____ Kate _____, we _____ _____ a baseball game.

3 네가 내일 이 시간에 나를 방문하면, 나는 내 차를 수리하고 있는 중일 거야. (repair)

When you visit me this time tomorrow, I _____ _____ _____ my
car.

4 나는 다음 주말에 부모님을 방문할 것이다. (visit)

I _____ _____ my parents next weekend.

5 Sally는 요즘 요리하는 방법을 배우고 있다. (learn, how to cook)

Sally _____ _____ _____ _____ _____ these days.

정답 및 해설 p.07

☑ **CHECK UP** 괄호 안에서 알맞은 것을 고르시오.

1 You (are having / have) a talent for music composition. `B`

2 It (is raining / rains) hard now. I'll stay home until it stops. `A-1`

3 Cats (are sleeping / sleep) 16 to 18 hours a day. `A-1`

4 I (am feeling / feel) that more people need to help poor children. `C-4`

5 What club (are you belonging / do you belong) to? `B`

A 괄호 안에 주어진 말을 현재시제 또는 현재진행형으로 바꾸어 빈칸에 쓰시오.

1 He often _____ to art galleries. (go)

2 Tom is outside. He _____ his motorbike. (wash)

3 Don't put the books away. I _____ them. (read)

4 Where is the ironing board? I _____ it. (need)

5 The Golden Gate Bridge _____ San Francisco and Marin County. (connect)

6 I _____ of buying a new computer. This one is outdated. (think)

B 보기에 주어진 말을 알맞은 형태로 바꾸어 빈칸에 쓰시오.

보기   flow   speak   look for   boil   know

1 Benny is very good at German. He _____ it fluently.

2 The soup _____. Can you turn off the stove?

3 The Amazon River _____ into the Atlantic Ocean.

4 I _____ the Lakeside Hotel. Could you show me the way?

5 Brian _____ that he needs to study hard to enter a good university.

C 다음 문장에서 어법상 틀린 곳을 찾아 고치시오. 틀린 곳이 없으면 O표 하시오.

1 She is liking to take pictures of flowers.

2 Kathy is thinking of moving out of her apartment.

3 I'm thinking that Sam is the most qualified for this position.

4 Do you believe in ghosts?

5 I can't talk to you about that now. I drive on the highway.

6 I'm not wanting to eat out tonight.

D **자연스러운 대화가 되도록 괄호 안에서 알맞은 것을 고르시오.**

1 A : What do you do after work?

B : I (usually relax / am usually relaxing) at home, but these days I'm learning how to play the guitar.

2 A : Wow, the soup (smells / is smelling) amazing!

B : Yes, it (tastes / is tasting) amazing, too.

3 A : How is your trip going?

B : I (have / am having) a great time!

WRITING PRACTICE

괄호 안의 말을 이용하여 영작을 완성하시오.

1 내가 생각하기에 그것이 네게 잘 어울리는 것 같아. (think, suit, you)

I _____ it _____ _____ well.

2 내가 듣기에 코끼리는 뛰어난 기억력을 가지고 있대. (have, amazing memories)

I heard that elephants _____ _____ _____.

3 Dan은 그 사고에 대해 죄책감을 느끼고 있다. (feel, guilty)

Dan _____ _____ _____ about the accident.

4 그 스마트폰은 Jane의 것이다. (belong)

The smartphone _____ _____ Jane.

5 달은 지구 주위를 약 한 달에 한 번 돈다. (go around)

The Moon _____ _____ the Earth about once a month.

☑ **CHECK UP** 괄호 안에서 알맞은 것을 고르시오.

1 Jean (has got / got) a new job last week.   `A-1`

2 Jack arrived in Spain last night, but he (hasn't called / didn't call) me yet.   `C`

3 (Do you read / Have you read) the novel already?   `C`

4 A: Can I speak to Mr. Field?   `B`

   B: Sorry, he (just leaves / has just left) for home.

A 다음 도표를 보고 Sam이 7시 이전에 한 일에는 already, 7시 이후 바로 한 일에는 just, 아직 안 했으면 yet을 사용하여 문장을 완성하시오.

▶ He has just had a cup of coffee. ▶ He hasn't got dressed yet. **1** He _____ . **2** He _____ . **3** He _____ . **4** He _____ .	It's 7:20 in the morning. * have a cup of coffee (7:05) * get dressed (×) * clean the kitchen (6:30) * read a newspaper (×) * water the plants (6:50) * make toast (7:15)

B 보기에 주어진 말을 알맞은 형태로 바꾸어 빈칸에 쓰시오. (현재완료를 이용할 것)

보기   arrive   break   lose   rise

1 Toby is looking for his wallet. He _____ it.

2 Joan can't walk. She _____ her leg.

3 This morning I was expecting a letter. Now I've got it. The letter _____ .

4 Last year the bus fare was 1,100 won. Now it's 1,200 won. The bus fare

   _____ .

C 주어진 말을 순서대로 활용하여 문장을 완성하시오.

Dear Sean,

Lots of things have happened since I phoned you last month.

0 I / just / buy / a new bicycle → I've just bought a new bicycle.

1 I / just / finish / an English composition course

→ _____ .

2 my father / not give up / smoking / yet

→ _____ .

3 my sisters / go / to France

→ _____ , so they aren't here now.

D 자연스러운 대화가 되도록 괄호 안에서 알맞은 것을 고르시오.

1 A : Can I use your phone for a second?

B : Oh, sorry. I (leave / have left) it in the car.

2 A : Is Samantha going to come to the fireworks display with us?

B : Oh, no. I (don't phone / haven't phoned) her yet.

WRITING PRACTICE

괄호 안의 말과 현재완료를 이용하여 영작을 완성하시오.

1 저 아직 결정하지 못했어요. (decide)

I _____ _____ yet.

2 나는 그 영화를 세 번 봤다. (watch)

I _____ _____ _____ _____ three times.

3 Harry는 지금까지 5년 동안 그 회사에 근무했다. (work for, company)

Harry _____ _____ _____ _____ _____ for five years.

4 나는 그의 번호를 잊어버려서 그에게 전화할 수 없다. (forget, number)

I _____ _____ _____ _____ , so I can't call him.

정답 및 해설 p.10

☑ **CHECK UP** 괄호 안에서 알맞은 것을 고르시오.

1 You are the greatest teacher I (ever meet / have ever met).   A-2

2 I've volunteered to help the homeless (for / since) 10 years.   B

3 Joe is on holiday. He has (gone / been) to Greece.   Upgrade Your Grammar

4 Have you ever (gone / been) to Moscow?   Upgrade Your Grammar

A 주어진 두 문장을 since 또는 for를 이용하여 한 문장으로 쓰시오.

0 I started to study Chinese in 2010. I still study Chinese.

→ I have studied Chinese since 2010.

1 Brad began to play the piano five years ago. He still plays the piano.

→ _____

2 I immigrated to Canada in 2014. I still live in Canada.

→ _____

3 I began to read comics when I was five years old. I still read comics.

→ _____

4 Teresa started to work for a TV station last year. She still works for it.

→ _____

B 보기에 주어진 말을 알맞은 형태로 바꾸어 빈칸에 쓰시오.

보기   eat   be   never/use   go   not/drive

1 These are so good. I _____ this kind of cookie before.

2 A : Can you drive?

B : Yes, but I _____ for a few years.

3 How many times _____ Jim _____ to Japan?

4 I don't know how to work this program. I _____ it before.

5 A : Where's Rebecca?

B : She _____ to the library.

C 다음 문장에서 어법상 틀린 곳을 찾아 바르게 고치시오. 틀린 곳이 없으면 ◯표 하시오.

1 I lived in this city since last year. I'll move to another city next year.

2 I have known David since many years.

3 He's been to New York to study. He's still there.

4 I've never seen such a beautiful model before. Who is she?

D 자연스러운 대화가 되도록 괄호 안에서 알맞은 것을 고르시오.

1 A : Where are Bill and Ben?

B : They (have gone / have been) shopping. They'll be back soon.

2 A : How long (do you live / have you lived) in Hong Kong?

B : I've lived here for three years.

3 A : Have you ever tried bungee jumping?

B : Sure! It was the most amazing thing (I experience / I've ever experienced).

WRITING PRACTICE

보기에 주어진 말을 이용하여 영작을 완성하시오.

보기	write	be	see	know	go

1 나는 3년째 그를 알고 지내고 있다.

I ＿＿＿＿＿＿ ＿＿＿＿＿＿ ＿＿＿＿＿＿ three years.

2 그것은 지금까지 내가 본 영화 중에서 가장 슬픈 영화였다.

It was ＿＿＿＿＿ ＿＿＿＿＿ ＿＿＿＿＿ I ＿＿＿＿＿ ＿＿＿＿＿ ＿＿＿＿＿.

3 내 남동생은 유럽에 한 번도 가 본 적이 없다.

My brother ＿＿＿＿＿ ＿＿＿＿＿ ＿＿＿＿＿ ＿＿＿＿＿ Europe.

4 그는 스무 살 때부터 5개의 영화 대본을 썼다.

He ＿＿＿＿＿ ＿＿＿＿＿ five movie scripts ＿＿＿＿＿ he was twenty.

5 Norton 씨는 출장으로 일본에 가고 없다.

Mr. Norton ＿＿＿＿＿ ＿＿＿＿＿ ＿＿＿＿＿ ＿＿＿＿＿ for a business trip.

☑ **CHECK UP**   괄호 안에서 알맞은 것을 고르시오.

1 I (visited / have visited) Peru when I was 8 years old.   `3 - f`

2 When (did you finish / have you finished) your report?   `7 - r`

3 The fax machine (jams / has jammed) again. Can you fix it?   `4 - g`

4 What time (have you gotten / did you get) to work this morning?   `6 - p`

A   괄호 안에 주어진 말을 과거시제 또는 현재완료형으로 바꾸어 빈칸에 쓰시오.

1 I _____ playing computer games for a few weeks, but now I'm playing them again. (stop)

2 I don't know much about Tom. I _____ to him. (never, talk)

3 I studied French at school, but I _____ most of it now. (forget)

4 The police _____ three people, but later they had to let them go. (arrest)

5 Ever since I _____ a child, I _____ afraid of crickets. (be)

B   다음 문장과 이어지는 질문을 읽고 보기와 같이 올바른 답에 O표 하시오.

0 Roger has left home.
  Q: Is Roger at home now?   (No.) / Don't know.

1 I made some cookies.
  Q: Are there cookies now?   Yes. / Don't know.

2 Clark went to China.
  Q: Is he still there now?   Yes. / Don't know.

3 Glen has gone to Madrid.
  Q: Is he there now?   Yes. / Don't know.

4 Katrina has started dance lessons.
  Q: Is she taking dance lessons now?   Yes. / Don't know.

C 다음 문장에서 어법상 <u>틀린</u> 곳을 찾아 고치시오. 틀린 곳이 없으면 O표 하시오.

1 My grandmother has grown up in Russia.

2 The couple have been married for 20 years.

3 Julie isn't at home. She's been to Guam for a change of scenery.

4 I have drunk four cups of coffee today.

5 Tina has made 13 films before she was killed in a car accident.

D 자연스러운 대화가 되도록 괄호 안에서 알맞은 것을 고르시오.

1 A : It's been 50 minutes, and the pizza still (didn't arrive / hasn't arrived).

   B : I'll call them and check on it.

2 A : When (did Justin move / has Justin moved) to California?

   B : He moved there last spring.

3 A : The weather is so dry.

   B : I know. It (didn't rain / hasn't rained) since last month.

WRITING PRACTICE

괄호 안의 말을 이용하여 영작을 완성하시오.

1 Emma는 런던에서 15년째 살고 있다. (live)

Emma _____ _____ _____ London _____ 15 years.

2 Alice는 어렸을 때 안경을 썼다. (wear glasses, be)

Alice _____ _____ _____ she _____ a child.

3 나는 3년 전에 팔이 부러졌지만, 그 후로는 팔에 문제가 없다. (break, have)

I _____ my arm 3 years ago, but I _____ _____ any problems with it since.

4 정부 당국자가 세금을 올리겠다는 계획들을 발표했다. (announce)

A government official _____ _____ _____ to raise taxes.

5 그녀는 출판사에 7년 근무했고, 지금은 게임 회사에 근무한다. (work for)

She _____ _____ a publishing company for seven years, and now she _____ _____ a gaming company.

UNIT 08 과거완료형, 미래완료형, 완료진행형

정답 및 해설 p.12

CHECK UP

괄호 안에서 알맞은 것을 고르시오.

1 When I got home, I realized that I (have left / had left) my wallet at the restaurant. `A-2`

2 She (has lived / will have lived) in Peru for two years next month. `B`

3 Jim (had been listening / has been listening) to a boring lecture for three hours, `C-2` so he started to fall asleep.

4 Matt (has been playing / will have been playing) hockey in the NHL for five years `C-3` next season.

A

다음을 읽고 질문에 알맞은 답을 고르시오.

1 When Rachel arrived to help me, I had already finished cleaning up.
Q: Which happened first?　　a. Rachel arrived.　　b. I cleaned up.

2 I had been there before, so I knew the way.
Q: Which happened first?　　a. I was there.　　b. I knew the way.

3 The presentation had ended, so I went outside.
Q: Which happened first?　　a. The presentation ended.　b. I went outside.

4 Steven had canceled his ticket before I decided not to go.
Q: Which happened first?　　a. my decision　　b. Steven's canceling

B

괄호 안에 주어진 말을 알맞은 시제의 완료형으로 변형하여 빈칸에 쓰시오.

1 Thomas didn't want to go to the museum with us as he _____ there. (already, be)

2 Meet me at 7:00 p.m. I _____ all my homework by then. (finish)

3 Helen works in Australia. She _____ in Australia for four years. (work)

4 The pipe was leaking. The landlord _____ it for years. (not, check)

C 밑줄 친 부분이 어법상 옳으면 O표 하고, 틀린 부분은 바르게 고치시오.

1 When I got home, my parents <u>have already gone</u> to bed.

2 Barry <u>has finished</u> the exams by this time tomorrow.

3 Clara <u>had been waiting</u> for three hours before the train arrived.

4 He <u>will be teaching</u> English in Singapore for 5 years next month.

D 주어진 문장을 읽고, 시제에 유의하여 완료진행형이 들어간 문장으로 바꿔 쓰시오.

1 The baby began to cry half an hour ago. He's still crying.

→ The baby _____.

2 He has worked for the company for 19 years. It's his 20th year anniversary next year.

→ He _____.

3 Paul and Jane started to date three months ago. They are still dating.

→ Paul and Jane _____.

WRITING PRACTICE

보기에 주어진 말을 이용하여 영작을 완성하시오.

보기	finish	get to	play	retire	start

1 내가 극장에 도착했을 때 영화는 이미 시작한 상태였다.

When I _____ _____ the theater, the movie _____ _____
_____ .

2 나는 내일 아침에는 그 보고서를 끝냈을 것이다.

I _____ _____ _____ the report by tomorrow morning.

3 비가 내리기 시작했을 때, 우리는 야구 경기를 하던 중이었다.

We _____ _____ _____ baseball when it started to rain.

4 내가 졸업할 때쯤이면, 우리 아버지는 은퇴하셨을 것이다.

By the time I graduate, my father _____ _____ _____ .

UNIT 09 can, could

정답 및 해설 p.14

↗ **CHECK UP** 괄호 안에서 알맞은 것을 고르시오.

1 I used to (can / be able to) stand on my head, but I can't do it now. `A·1`

2 The students (could / were able to) pass the exam after studying hard. `A·1`

3 You (can / are able to) use my laptop computer whenever you want. `A·2`

4 (Can it be / Is it able to be) right to keep silent? `A·4`

5 The doorbell's ringing. It (could / was able to) be Vincent. `B·2`

6 Cell phones (can / are able to) be used as voice recorders, too. `A·3`

A can[can't] 또는 be able to를 빈칸에 알맞은 형태로 쓰시오. (둘 다 가능한 경우 can[can't]을 쓸 것)

1 Gary is really interested in music. He _____ play many instruments.

2 He _____ be the bridegroom. He's just twelve.

3 You _____ get some information at the tourist center.

4 Go to Professor Smith and ask. He might _____ help you.

5 I don't understand Laura's behavior. I've never _____ predict it.

B 밑줄 친 can의 의미가 같은 것끼리 연결하고 보기에서 그 의미를 찾아 쓰시오.

보기	능력	가능	허가 및 요청	추측

1 Nell can play the piano.

2 Can I return the book this Friday?

3 They haven't lived here for very long. They can't know many people.

4 It can happen to anybody.

a. You've just had lunch. You can't be hungry already.

b. Spring can be very cold sometimes.

c. Can I take one of these bananas?

d. Jody can't speak Japanese well.

1 _____ ( )   **2** _____ ( )

3 _____ ( )   **4** _____ ( )

C   다음 문장에서 어법상 <u>틀린</u> 곳을 찾아 고치시오. 틀린 곳이 없으면 O표 하시오.

1   Andy can't be at home. His car is gone.

2   Aaron missed the last bus, but luckily he can get a ride from a stranger.

3   I couldn't swim until I was 15, but now I'm a strong swimmer.

4   It's nice to can go to the concert with you.

D   괄호 안에 주어진 말과 can[could] 또는 can't[couldn't]를 이용하여 빈칸을 채우시오.

1   A : I'm sorry I _____ (help) you with your project.

  B : It's okay. I will be able to manage somehow.

2   A : You _____ (use) the company car while you're visiting.

  B : Thank you.

3   A : The zoo was closed, so we _____ (take) pictures of the tigers.

  B : That's too bad.

WRITING **PRACTICE**

괄호 안의 말을 이용하여 영작을 완성하시오.

1   스마트폰은 중독성이 있을 수 있다. (addictive)

Smartphones _____ _____ _____.

2   그가 그 사고를 목격했을 리가 없어. (witness)

He _____ _____ _____ the accident.

3   당신의 옷을 이번 주 금요일까지 배송할 수 있을 것입니다. (will)

I _____ _____ _____ _____ deliver your clothes by this
Friday.

4   Jane은 트럭에 부딪히기 전에 그녀의 차를 멈출 수 있었다. (stop)

Jane _____ _____ _____ _____ her car before crashing
into the truck.

5   각각의 승객은 비행기에 하나의 가방을 가지고 탑승할 수 있습니다. (passenger, take)

Each _____ _____ _____ one bag onto the plane.

☑ **CHECK UP** 괄호 안에서 알맞은 것을 고르시오.

1 Take sunglasses with you. It (may be / may have been) sunny today. `A-3`

2 You (may well / may as well) want to quit, but you shouldn't. `A-5`

3 Jim looked so tired. He (may not sleep / might not have slept) last night. `B-2`

4 (May / Might) you be happy with your family! `A-4`

A 밑줄 친 may의 의미가 같은 것끼리 연결하고 보기에서 그 의미를 찾아 쓰시오.

보기   허가 및 요청   현재나 미래의 추측·가능성   기원   과거 사실의 추측

1 You may help yourself to something to drink.	a. Gary may be coming tonight.
2 May you have every success in the future!	b. May I get myself a coffee?
3 It may sound odd, but I really saw a UFO.	c. Joe may not have heard me properly.
4 Sam may have arrived late.	d. May good fortune be with you!

1 _____ (   ) **2** _____ (   )

3 _____ (   ) **4** _____ (   )

B may 또는 may have v-ed를 이용하여 대화를 완성하시오.

1 A : Why isn't Trevor coming?

    B : He _____. (be feeling ill)

2 A : Why is Claire so gloomy?

    B : She _____ with her boyfriend again. (have an argument)

3 A : Why is Hal late again?

    B : He _____. (miss his train)

C 보기에 주어진 말과 may well 또는 may as well을 이용하여 문장을 완성하시오.

보기   wait   take a bus   be annoyed   rain

1 With this traffic, a taxi would be no quicker. We _____.

2 The restaurant isn't open yet. We _____ at a café.

3 Linda took Dan's jacket again. Dan _____.

4 Look at those dark clouds. It _____ soon.

D 자연스러운 대화가 되도록 괄호 안에서 알맞은 것을 고르시오.

1 A : May I borrow your pen?

　　B : Of course you (can / might).

2 A : I (might be able to / might have been able to) meet you today.

　　B : That's great. Give me a call later.

3 A : I'm feeling sick, so I (may / may not) be able to go to school today.

　　B : I'm sorry to hear that. Stay home and take care of yourself.

WRITING PRACTICE

괄호 안의 말을 이용하여 영작을 완성하시오.

1 그녀는 이 모임에 대해 모를지도 몰라. (might, know)

She _____ _____ _____ about this meeting.

2 그가 두 개 이상의 언어를 말한다는 것은 당연하다. (may, speak)

He _____ _____ _____ more than two languages.

3 만약 아무도 그것을 원치 않으면 그녀에게 주는 것이 낫다. (may, give)

If no one wants it, we _____ _____ _____ _____ it to her.

4 Irene은 아직 내 메시지를 받지 않았을지도 모르겠어. (might, receive)

Irene _____ _____ _____ _____ my message yet.

5 일부 사용자들이 오늘 아침 로그인 문제를 경험했을지도 모릅니다. (may, experience)

Some users _____ _____ _____ login issues this morning.

UNIT 11 will, would, shall

정답 및 해설 p.16

⤷ **CHECK UP**   괄호 안에서 알맞은 것을 고르시오.

1 How long (will / shall) you be staying in Paris?   `A-1`

2 When I was a child, I (would / shall) climb the tree in the backyard.   `B-3`

3 Sean promised that he (would / shall) visit her the next day.   `B-4`

4 The plant (will / would like to) die without water.   `A-4`

5 (Shall / Would) we go to the concert on Saturday?   `C-1`

A

will 또는 shall을 이용하여 대화를 완성하시오.

Joey   : What _____ we do today?

Rachel : It would be nice to go out somewhere. The weather forecast says it _____ be sunny and warm today.

Ross   : _____ we just stay at home and watch an NBA game? The forecast _____ probably be wrong again. Look at the clouds.

Phoebe : Come on Ross! What about going to the amusement park? It _____ be fun!

Joey   : How much _____ it cost? I'm low on money.

Tommy   : Don't worry! I _____ pay for you as usual.

Rachel : Okay. _____ we leave Ross at home to watch TV alone?

Ross   : No. If everyone's going, I guess I _____ go, too.

B

보기에 주어진 말과 will, would, shall을 이용하여 문장을 완성하시오.

보기	stop	meet	get fat	drink

1 _____ I _____ you as soon as you finish work?

2 I _____ biting my fingernails from now on.

3 My grandfather _____ often _____ a glass of whiskey after dinner when he was younger.

4 You _____ if you eat a lot of candy.

C   다음 문장에서 어법상 <u>틀린</u> 곳을 찾아 고치시오. 틀린 곳이 없으면 O표 하시오.

1 They told me that they will come, but they never showed up.

2 I'm tired. Will we just stay at home tonight?

3 It's no use talking to Jimmy. He wouldn't understand.

4 Shall you come with me?

5 Natural rubber will stretch easily when pulled.

D   자연스러운 대화가 되도록 괄호 안에서 알맞은 것을 고르시오.

1 A : (Will / Shall) you take a message?

   B : No problem.

2 A : My parents said they (would / shall) take me to a ballpark.

   B : That's awesome!

3 A : (Will / Would) you like to have some tea?

   B : Yes, please.

WRITING PRACTICE

괄호 안의 말을 이용하여 영작을 완성하시오.

1 제가 언제 다시 당신을 방문하면 될까요? (shall, visit, again)

When _____ ?

2 나는 저녁을 먹고 나서 내 애완견과 산책하곤 했다. (would, take)

After dinner, I _____ with my dog.

3 우리는 이 경기에서 이기기 위해 최선을 다할 것이다. (will, do one's best)

We _____ to win this game.

4 그녀는 내게 그 책을 돌려주겠다고 말했는데, 그러지 않았다. (would, give, back)

She said that _____ to me but she didn't.

5 그것은 하기에 쉬운 일이 아닐 것이다. (would, thing)

It _____ to do.

UNIT 12 must, have to, should, ought to

☑ **CHECK UP** 괄호 안에서 알맞은 것을 고르시오.

1 I have a terrible toothache so I (must not / don't have to) eat any candy. `A-2`

2 This puppy will (must / have to) get shots. `A-1`

3 I (shouldn't talk / shouldn't have talked) with her. I was tricked into telling my secret. `B-1`

4 She insisted that I (dance / danced) even though I didn't know how. `C-1`

5 I picked up the smartphone. Someone (had to leave / must have left) it behind. `A-3`

A must 또는 have to를 빈칸에 알맞은 형태로 쓰시오. (둘 다 가능한 경우 must를 쓸 것)

1 Fred _____ leave for home before it got dark.

2 People _____ not park by the hospital entrance.

3 You don't _____ attend the weekly meeting if you're busy.

4 The students will _____ finish their science projects by tomorrow.

5 He has been working for 10 hours. He _____ be exhausted.

6 Her car is gone, so she _____ have left already.

B 보기에 주어진 말과 should 또는 should have v-ed를 이용하여 빈칸을 완성하시오.

> 보기   see   get some sleep   come   get up   not / go jogging

1 Michael has hurt his ankle. He _____ in the rain.

2 I have a sore throat and a stuffy nose. I _____ a doctor.

3 The exhibition was really interesting. You _____ along.

4 Diana was late for class again today. She _____ earlier.

5 Jill is very tired at the moment. She _____.

C 밑줄 친 부분에 주의하여 다음 문장을 해석하시오.

1 You <u>must not exceed</u> the speed limit.

2 I <u>suggested that he join</u> the army next year.

3 We <u>shouldn't have bought</u> the car.

D 자연스러운 대화가 되도록 괄호 안에서 알맞은 것을 고르시오.

1 A : Lucy won't talk to me. What should I do?

B : You (ought to call / must have called) her and say sorry.

2 A : What can I do to help the environment?

B : It's important that you (tried / should try) to reduce waste whenever possible.

3 A : John insists that he (shouldn't do / didn't do) anything wrong.

B : He never admits his mistakes.

4 A : How old is Ron?

B : He's quite a lot older than you. He (must be / must have been) at least 35.

WRITING PRACTICE

보기에 주어진 말을 이용하여 영작을 완성하시오.

보기	pay	judge	insist	practice	support

1 나는 그 대회를 위해 더 연습을 했어야 했으나 하지 않았다.

I _____ _____ _____ more for the contest, but I didn't.

2 그는 우리가 James의 사업을 지원해야 한다고 주장했다.

_____ _____ we _____ James's business.

3 5세 미만의 어린이는 입장료를 낼 필요가 없다.

Children under five don't _____ _____ _____ an entrance fee.

4 우리는 사람을 외모로 판단하면 안 된다.

We _____ _____ _____ _____ people by their appearance.

⊿ **CHECK UP** 괄호 안에서 알맞은 것을 고르시오.

1 When I was a child, I (used to / am used to) ride a bike every day.　　A

2 You (had better / would rather) go now, or you will be late again.　　B - 1

3 I (had better / would rather) walk home than take a crowded bus.　　B - 2

4 There (used to / would) be a second-hand store on that corner.　　Upgrade Your Grammar

5 We (don't need talk / need not talk) about it right now.　　C

A 괄호 안에 주어진 말과 used to-v, be used to-v 또는 be used to v-ing을 이용하여 빈칸을 완성 하시오.

1 When I was young, I _____ the ducks in our local pond. (feed)

2 Life jackets _____ lives. (save)

3 I _____, so I usually eat out. (not / cook)

4 I _____ very thin, but I have gained a lot of weight lately. (look)

5 Ronny _____ early, so meeting at 7:00 a.m. will be no problem for him. (wake up)

B 보기에 주어진 말과 had better 또는 would rather를 이용하여 빈칸을 완성하시오.

보기	go	tell	have	visit	start	give up

1 I _____ on the test than cheat.

2 I _____ to bed early. I'm not in the mood to meet people.

3 I have to catch a plane tonight. I _____ packing now.

4 You _____ the truth, or I will.

5 Anita will be angry if we disturb her, so we _____ her later.

6 _____ you _____ Korean food for dinner tonight?

C 밑줄 친 부분이 어법상 옳으면 O표 하고, 틀린 부분은 바르게 고치시오.

1 I <u>had better not tell</u> him the story. He will be worried.

2 They <u>don't need pay</u> any money to see the show.

3 My grandparents <u>aren't used to live</u> in a big city.

4 I <u>would rather not wear</u> those pants. They make me look fat.

5 There <u>would be</u> an old bookstore that a stubborn old man ran.

D 괄호 안의 말을 알맞게 배열하여 문장을 완성하시오.

1 (used to, I, basketball, play) a lot. Now I play golf.

2 (the movies, I, go to, than, would rather) stay at home alone.

3 It's getting late. (going, think about, we, had better) home.

4 (you, to, wear, need, in bright sunlight, sunglasses) to protect your eyes.

WRITING PRACTICE

괄호 안의 말을 이용하여 영작을 완성하시오.

1 나는 노래를 부르느니 춤을 추겠다. (dance, sing)

I _____ _____ _____ _____ _____.

2 Jim은 크리스마스 때마다 이 고아원을 방문하곤 했나요? (visit)

_____ Jim _____ _____ _____ this orphanage every Christmas?

3 너는 너의 운전 면허증을 경찰에게 보여주는 것이 낫겠다. (show)

You _____ _____ _____ your driver's license to the police.

4 너는 모든 질문에 답할 필요가 없다. (answer)

You _____ _____ _____ all the questions.

5 카카오 열매는 초콜릿을 만드는 데 사용된다. (to, make)

Cacao beans _____ _____ _____ _____ chocolate.

↗ **CHECK UP** 괄호 안에서 알맞은 것을 고르시오.

1 I (was able to / could) win the race, so I got a medal. 능력

2 The restaurant is famous for its steak. You (had better / should) go there. 충고·권유

3 He knows a lot about the book. He (must / can't) have read it. 과거의 추정

4 She (can't / must) be an artist. She is not good at painting. 추측

A 보기에서 알맞은 것을 골라 빈칸에 쓰시오.

보기　can't have been　might have closed　couldn't see　must be　ought to look

1 Mark and Peter have the same surname and look alike. They _____ brothers.

2 I haven't eaten in the restaurant for a while. It _____ down.

3 When you buy milk, you _____ at the expiration date on it.

4 It _____ easy for him to leave his family and friends behind.

5 I was sitting in the back row, so I _____ the actors well.

B 다음 대화를 읽고 B의 대답이 의미하는 것을 고르시오.

1 A : Why isn't Martin at school today?

　B : Well, he may be sick.

　　a. I'm sure he's sick.　　　　　　　　b. I'm not sure, but I think he's sick.

2 A : Can I see the recording of the documentary?

　B : I can't find it. I might not have recorded it.

　　a. I'm not sure if I recorded it.　　　　b. I certainly didn't record it.

3 A : Did you see the game?

　B : They should have played better.

　　a. They played well.　　　　　　　　b. They didn't play well enough.

C 다음 중 문맥과 어법상 빈칸에 들어갈 수 <u>없는</u> 것을 고르시오.

1 It looks like rain. You _____ the windows.
   a. should shut   b. ought to shut   c. had better shut   d. would shut

2 There is someone at the door. It _____ Sammy.
   a. must be   b. might be   c. used to be   d. could be

3 In Korea, elementary education is compulsory. All children _____ six years of elementary school.
   a. are able to attend   b. have to attend   c. must attend   d. need to attend

D 괄호 안의 말을 이용하여 대화를 완성하시오.

1 A : Why isn't Ann here yet? She is 30 minutes late.
   B : She _____ lost. (may, get)

2 A : You _____ Thai food some time. (ought, try) It's really good.
   B : Is it? Do you know a good place to try it?

3 A : Whose bag is this?
   B : Polly _____ it here. (must, leave)

WRITING PRACTICE

괄호 안의 말을 이용하여 영작을 완성하시오.

1 나는 멀리서도 그녀를 알아볼 수 있었다. (recognize)

I _____ _____ _____ _____ her from a distance.

2 그는 그의 모든 돈을 자선금으로 기부했음이 틀림없다. (donate)

He _____ _____ _____ all his money to charity.

3 Sue가 지난주의 그 사고를 목격했을지도 모른다. (witness)

Sue _____ _____ _____ the accident last week.

4 서두르는 게 좋겠다. 아니면 비행기를 놓칠 거야. (hurry)

We _____ _____ _____, or we will miss the flight.

UNIT 15 수동태의 기본 개념 및 형태

정답 및 해설 p.22

☑ CHECK UP 괄호 안에서 알맞은 것을 고르시오.

1 Many accidents (are caused by / cause) drunken drivers.　　　`A`

2 He (lacked / was lacked) a sense of humor, and didn't understand jokes.　`D-2`

3 The sun (is risen / rises) in the East and (is set / sets) in the West.　`D-1`

4 We (were woken up by / are woken up by) loud music last night.　`B-1`

5 This house (was built / built) in 1897.　　　`C`

A 다음 능동태 문장을 수동태로 바꾸시오.

0 This charity helps poor children every year.

　→ Poor children are helped by this charity every year.

1 Martha took my calculator.

　→ _____

2 Somebody accused me of stealing money.

　→ _____

3 Students don't use this library often.

　→ _____

4 The government postponed all public events because of the weather.

　→ _____

B 괄호 안에 주어진 말을 빈칸에 알맞은 형태로 쓰시오.

1 The meeting will _____ in London next week. (hold)

2 I want a hotel that _____ downtown. (locate)

3 Many people _____ during the last hurricane. (kill)

4 He _____ when the scandal broke. (disappear)

5 Their bread _____ here every morning. (bake)

6 The roof of the building _____ in a storm a few days ago. (damage)

C 다음 문장에서 어법상 <u>틀린</u> 곳을 찾아 고치시오. 틀린 곳이 없으면 O표 하시오.

1 Because a recent flood damaged the road, it repaired yesterday.

2 How many concerts held at the university last year?

3 I don't think this coat really suits me.

4 The police was arrested the man for identity theft.

5 The telephone invented by Alexander Graham Bell in 1876.

D 자연스러운 대화가 되도록 괄호 안에서 알맞은 것을 고르시오.

1 A : Brice looks like his brother.

B : Yes, they (resemble / are resembled) each other a lot.

2 A : Do you know when the next train (arrives / is arrived)?

B : It will be here in a few minutes.

3 A : It's quite cold in here.

B : Well, it looks like one of the windows (breaks / is broken).

WRITING PRACTICE

괄호 안의 말을 이용하여 영작을 완성하시오.

1 그는 돈을 훔친 것에 대해 벌을 받았다. (punish)

He _____ _____ for stealing the money.

2 내 동생이 차에 치여 다쳤다. (hit)

My brother _____ _____ _____ a car and injured.

3 월드컵은 4년에 한 번씩 치러지니? (hold, every, four, years)

_____ the World Cup _____ _____ _____ _____ ?

4 원자력은 전력 생산에 사용된다. (use, to produce, electricity)

Nuclear energy _____ _____ _____ _____ _____ .

5 그 방문객들은 여행사 직원에 의해 공항까지 태워졌다. (drive, to the airport)

The visitors _____ _____ _____ _____ _____ by their travel agent.

정답 및 해설 p.23

↗ **CHECK UP** 괄호 안에서 알맞은 것을 고르시오.

1 There's somebody behind us. I think we (are following / are being followed). `A`

2 My father (had been taken / will be taken) to the hospital before I came home. `B`

3 This report (must finish / must be finished) before this Wednesday. `C`

4 Please leave me alone. I don't want to (disturb / be disturbed). `D`

5 He didn't mind (criticizing / being criticized) by the public. `E`

A 괄호 안에 주어진 말을 빈칸에 알맞은 형태로 쓰시오.

1 This card game should _____ with four people. (play)

2 Nobody likes _____ advantage of. (take)

3 New labor acts _____ recently. (have enforced)

4 If you want _____ like an adult, start acting like one. (treat)

B 다음 능동태 문장을 수동태로 바꾸시오.

0 The manager has fired three workers this week.

   → Three workers have been fired by the manager this week.

1 She will have written the emails by tomorrow.

   → The emails _____ by tomorrow.

2 They are making new rules for safe driving.

   → New rules for _____.

3 Has Tim formed a new band?

   → _____ by Tim?

4 Some animals can understand humans.

   → Humans _____.

C 다음 문장에서 어법상 <u>틀린</u> 곳을 찾아 고치시오. 틀린 곳이 없으면 O표 하시오.

1 The windows were washing while I was walking by the building.

2 The winner may keep the trophy for one year.

3 I remember be losing in a department store when I was young.

4 A number of political prisoners have released lately.

5 Will the first presentation be given by Nathan?

D 빈칸에 들어갈 말로 가장 알맞은 것을 고르시오.

1 My computer _____ recently. It works well now.

① has repaired　　　　② be repaired　　　　③ being repaired

④ was been repaired　　⑤ has been repaired

2 The grass in the yard _____ now, so it's very noisy outside.

① is cutting　　　　② being cut　　　　③ is being cut

④ will be cut　　　　⑤ had been cut

3 The water in the fish tank _____ regularly.

① cleans　　　　② is cleaning　　　　③ to be cleaned

④ has cleaned　　⑤ must be cleaned

WRITING PRACTICE

괄호 안의 말을 이용하여 영작을 완성하시오.

1 기계는 안전을 위해 정기적으로 점검을 받아야 한다. (should, check)

The machine _____ _____ _____ regularly for safety.

2 나는 외출하기 전에 날씨에 관해 경고받았었다. (have, warn)

I _____ _____ _____ about the weather before I went out.

3 모든 놀라운 발명품들은 실리적인 목적을 위해 만들어져 왔다. (have, make)

All amazing inventions _____ _____ _____ for practical purposes.

4 Rosie는 끼어드는 것을 그만두라고 타일러져야 한다. (have to, tell)

Rosie _____ _____ _____ _____ to stop interrupting.

☑ **CHECK UP** 괄호 안에서 알맞은 것을 고르시오.

1 The information (was given / was given to) a secret agency. `A-1`

2 The wedding cake (was made for / was made to) this young couple. `A-2`

3 This dress (was made popular / was made to popular) by an actress. `B`

4 The puppy (was looked / was looked after) by my brother. `C`

A 다음 문장을 괄호 안의 명사를 주어로 하여 수동태로 바꾸시오.

0 My grandmother gave me the old music box.

→ I was given the old music box by my grandmother. (me)

→ The old music box was given to me by my grandmother. (the old music box)

1 The company offered Jack the position.

→ _____ (Jack)

→ _____ (the position)

2 My boyfriend bought me this coat.

→ _____ (this coat)

3 My father will teach me the history of Korea.

→ _____ (me)

→ _____ (the history of Korea)

B 다음 능동태를 수동태로, 수동태를 능동태로 고치시오. (행위자를 밝힐 필요 없으면 생략)

1 We didn't see her leave the house.

→ _____

2 He was referred to as "the boss" by everyone.

→ _____

3 You should pick up this trash.

→ _____

4 The match was called off by the police for reasons of public safety.

→ _____

C 다음 문장에서 어법상 틀린 곳을 찾아 고치시오. 틀린 곳이 없으면 O표 하시오.

1 I wasn't given to the correct phone number.

2 He is considered an expert in biology.

3 His jokes are always laughed at his friends.

4 Some students are made take extra classes.

D 괄호 안에 주어진 말을 빈칸에 알맞은 형태로 쓰시오.

1 She was _____ to be a difficult person. (think)

2 Were the flowers _____ to Claire? (give)

3 We are not allowed _____ video games at home. (play)

4 People were heard _____ up the stairs every night. (walk)

WRITING PRACTICE

괄호 안의 말을 이용하여 영작을 완성하시오.

1 Cecil은 부통령으로 선출되었다. (elect, vice president)

Cecil _____ _____ _____ _____.

2 이 파일은 James에게 곧장 보내져야 한다. (should, send)

This file _____ _____ _____ _____ James directly.

3 나는 저녁 식사 후에 설거지를 하게 되었다. (make, do the dishes)

I _____ _____ _____ _____ _____ _____
after dinner.

4 그 화분은 내가 내 어머니를 위해 산 것이다. (buy)

The potted plant _____ _____ _____ _____
by me.

5 그 사건의 조사는 경찰에 의해 곧 이뤄질 것이다. (carry out)

An investigation into the accident will _____ _____ _____
_____ the police soon.

UNIT 18 다양한 수동태 표현

정답 및 해설 p.26

☑ **CHECK UP**   괄호 안에서 알맞은 것을 고르시오.

1 Victor was involved (in / to) a hit-and-run accident.   `A-2`

2 She (is said that / is said to) volunteer 15 hours a week.   `B`

3 Your pants need (washing / washed).   `C`

4 (It / That) is said that dogs are loyal.   `B`

A   빈칸에 들어갈 말을 보기에서 골라 쓰고 각 문장을 해석하시오.

보기   peel   needs   blame   selling

1 Hard-boiled eggs usually _____ easily.

2 Nobody is to _____ for what happened.

3 His new book is _____ like hotcakes.

4 My camera is broken. It _____ repairing.

B   괄호 안에 주어진 말을 빈칸에 알맞은 형태로 쓰시오.

1 The presentation is _____ _____ four sections. (compose)

2 I am _____ _____ my progress. (satisfy)

3 They were not _____ _____ having to wait so long. (surprise)

4 The room was _____ _____ smoke. (fill)

5 Mary is _____ _____ learning to play the piano. (interest)

C   주어진 문장과 같은 뜻이 되도록 문장을 다시 쓰시오.

0 He was said to be a very sincere person.

→ It was said that he was a very sincere person.

1 He is thought to have been the greatest authority on ancient Egypt.

→ It _____.

2 It is expected that the weather will improve over the next few weeks.

   → The weather _____ .

3 It was believed that the politician had taken a bribe.

   → The politician _____ .

D　**우리말과 일치하도록 괄호 안의 말을 바르게 배열하시오.**

1 그녀는 자기 회사에서 정보를 훔쳤다고 보도되었다.

(to, was, reported, she, have stolen, information) from her company.

2 Sarah는 비밀 요원이라고 믿어진다.

(it, is, is, Sarah, believed, that) a secret agent.

3 다행히도 그녀는 새로운 절차에 익숙하다.

Luckily, (is, she, the new procedures, accustomed to).

WRITING PRACTICE

괄호 안의 말을 이용하여 영작을 완성하시오.

1 그의 최신작은 잘 팔리고 있다. (sell, well)

His latest book _____ _____ _____ .

2 그 백화점은 쇼핑객으로 붐볐다. (crowd)

The department store _____ _____ _____ shoppers.

3 Nicole이 Jack과 사귀었다는 이야기가 있다. (say, go out)

Nicole _____ _____ to _____ _____ _____ with
Jack.

4 그 길은 눈으로 덮여 있었다. (cover, snow)

The street _____ _____ _____ _____ .

5 고양이는 개보다 훈련하는 것이 어렵다고 여겨진다. (think)

It _____ _____ _____ _____ _____ harder to train
than dogs.

실전 TEST 01 Chapter 01-03

1 빈칸에 알맞은 것을 고르시오.

> The fact will be known _____ everyone in your class.

① for ② of ③ to
④ in ⑤ as

2 괄호 안의 말을 각각 알맞은 형태로 쓰시오.

> A: Jim doesn't look good these days.
> B: He's been depressed since last week.
> A: What ⓐ (happen)?
> B: He ⓑ (fire) from his job.

3 다음 중 어법상 맞는 것을 고르시오.

① What time was your flight arrived?
② He isn't suited by the blue shirt.
③ Identical twins are resembled.
④ The class will be finished in a moment.
⑤ The ship was disappeared in the fog.

4 다음 중 어법상 <u>틀린</u> 것을 고르시오.

① Water consists of hydrogen and oxygen.
② Excuse me, is this seat taken?
③ The Internet uses as a communication tool.
④ I'm honored to work with you.
⑤ This monthly magazine sells well.

5 다음 문장을 수동태로 바꿀 때, 빈칸에 알맞은 말을 쓰시오.

> They bought me this birthday cake.
> → This birthday cake _____
> _____ me.

6 우리말을 영어로 바르게 옮기지 <u>못한</u> 것을 고르시오.

> 영어는 배우기 쉽다고 사람들은 말한다.

① English is said to be easy to learn.
② It is said that English is easy to learn.
③ People say that English is easy to learn.
④ English is said that it is easy to learn.
⑤ People say that it is easy to learn English.

7 빈칸에 공통으로 들어갈 조동사를 쓰시오.

> (A) How _____ it be true? I don't believe it.
> (B) You _____ use my cell phone.
> (C) She _____ cook well, but she rarely has the time.

8 다음 중 조동사의 쓰임이 <u>어색한</u> 것을 고르시오.

① He might not come back tomorrow.
② You don't have to violate the speed limit. It's illegal.
③ You look very tired. You can go home.
④ We may as well get used to it. It's not going to change.
⑤ He's stubborn. He won't listen to me.

9 [보기]의 would와 의미가 같은 것을 고르시오.

> [보기] I would go to church on Sundays
> when I was in high school.

① Would you like a cup of coffee?
② He said he would finish it.
③ They wouldn't sell the car.
④ It would be fun to throw a party.
⑤ He would read many books when he was
a child.

10 밑줄 친 문장을 우리말로 옮기시오.

> A : I wonder why she didn't keep her
> promise.
> B : She may have forgotten about it.

11 우리말을 영어로 바르게 옮긴 것을 고르시오.

> 그가 그 소식을 듣고 기뻤을 리가 없다.

① He cannot have been pleased to hear the
news.
② He couldn't be pleased to hear the news.
③ He must not have been pleased to hear
the news.
④ He might not have been pleased to hear
the news.
⑤ He should not have been pleased to hear
the news.

[12-13] 빈칸에 들어갈 수 없는 것을 고르시오.

12

> A : _____ you lend me some
> money?
> B : Sure. How much do you need?

① Will   ② Would   ③ May
④ Can   ⑤ Could

13

> You _____ go to bed now, or
> you will be tired tomorrow.

① must   ② used to   ③ should
④ ought to   ⑤ have to

14 다음 중 need의 쓰임이 바른 것을 고르시오.

① He needs not make money.
② Do I need to say it again?
③ He doesn't need go to a bank.
④ We need go home right now.
⑤ Does he needs to study harder?

15 어법상 어색한 곳을 찾아 고치시오. (1개)

> I lost 15 pounds. I could do it by walking
> and swimming a lot. I was not satisfied
> with my body, but now I'm happy with
> how I look.

16 다음 중 어법상 틀린 것을 모두 고르시오.

① You'd better not go there.
② She won the award. She must prepare a lot.
③ This used to be a playground.
④ I won't wait if you will be late.
⑤ The witness insisted that he had heard the gunshot.

17 [보기]의 밑줄 친 부분과 쓰임이 같은 것을 고르시오.

[보기] How many times have you been to New York?

① They have been happily married for 30 years.
② It was the most exciting movie I have ever seen.
③ I haven't decided yet if I want to go to college.
④ We have worked on this project for a month.
⑤ The deer has run away from the hunters.

18 빈칸에 들어갈 수 없는 것을 고르시오.

I _____ tomorrow morning.

① will leave   ② leave
③ am leaving   ④ am going to leave
⑤ have left

19 두 문장이 같은 의미가 되도록 빈칸에 알맞은 말을 쓰시오.

He started playing baseball this morning. He is still playing.
→ He _____ _____ _____ baseball since this morning.

20 다음 대화문에서 밑줄 친 부분이 어색한 것을 고르시오.

① A : He is really good at math.
   B : You're right. I'm believing he is a genius.
② A : Why did you leave last night?
   B : I was having a terrible time at the party.
③ A : What are you doing?
   B : I'm tasting the chicken soup.
④ A : How are you feeling today?
   B : Not bad.
⑤ A : What will you do this weekend?
   B : I'm thinking of going to a museum.

21 어법상 어색한 곳을 찾아 고치시오. (1개)

He has served as a police officer for 20 years. But he got fired a couple of years ago because he was involved in drug trafficking.

22 밑줄 친 부분이 어법상 맞는 것을 모두 고르시오.

① She is smelling flowers she got from her friend.
② I'm hating to stay home on the weekend.
③ This book is belonging to me.
④ I was having lunch when you called me.
⑤ I am needing help with writing my essay.

[23-24] 다음 글을 읽고, 물음에 답하시오.

The other night when our parents were out, my little brother and I got into a little fight. It wasn't that bad, but I got angry and broke his phone, which I ① shouldn't do. He started to talk about how he ② was going to tell our parents and get me in trouble. I didn't want ③ to be scolded. So I grabbed him by the arm and said, "If you ④ tell on me, I will take your allowance." However, he didn't care. He just said he ⑤ would tell and get me in trouble.

23 위 글의 내용과 일치하는 것을 고르시오.

① 부모님이 자고 있을 때 동생과 싸웠다.
② 동생이 내 휴대 전화를 망가뜨렸다.
③ 동생이 부모님께 이르려고 했다.
④ 나는 부모님께 혼이 났다.
⑤ 동생은 나의 말에 겁을 먹었다.

24 ①~⑤ 중 어법상 틀린 것을 고르시오.

①   ②   ③   ④   ⑤

[25-27] 다음 글을 읽고, 물음에 답하시오.

There's another similar case. In 2006, a problem occurred with a family that ⓐ (has / had) recently moved to America. The father got angry with his son and punished him by hitting him with a stick. A teacher later noticed the black-and-blue marks on the boy's legs and called the police. Such a punishment was acceptable in the family's old country, but in America the father ⓑ (arrested / was arrested). When the boy's father was finally released from prison, he ① (make) attend a special class to learn how to take proper care of his son.

25 위 글 앞에 나올 내용으로 가장 알맞은 것을 고르시오.

① 문화 차이로 인한 이민자의 고충
② 나라마다 다른 아버지의 사랑
③ 학교 교육의 문제점과 대안
④ 적정한 처벌의 필요성
⑤ 이민자가 급증하고 있는 이유

26 ⓐ, ⓑ의 괄호 안에서 어법상 맞는 것을 고르시오.

27 괄호 ①의 (make)를 어법에 맞게 쓰시오.

→ _____

UNIT 19 명사처럼 쓰이는 to부정사 I

☑ **CHECK UP** 괄호 안에서 알맞은 것을 고르시오.

1 Is it dangerous (to wear not / not to wear) long pants in the rain forest?　　B-3

2 The purpose of this group is (to oppose / oppose) the government's education policy.　　A-3 C

3 (To do exercise / Do exercise) every day is really good for your health.　　A-1

4 All I want to do is just (goes to bed / go to bed).　　C

A　to부정사에 밑줄을 긋고, 주어, 목적어, 주격 보어 중 어떤 역할을 하는지 쓰시오.

1 I think it's safe to cross the street.　　[　　　　]

2 It's very hard not to eat fast food.　　[　　　　]

3 My idea is to find a pretty beach.　　[　　　　]

4 The union decided to go on strike.　　[　　　　]

B　주어진 말을 알맞게 배열하여 문장을 완성하시오. (필요한 경우 to부정사를 이용할 것)

0 it / impossible / to the past / go back / is

　→ It is impossible to go back to the past.

1 was / his jokes / not laugh at / it / hard

　→ _____

2 my sister's / is / ambition / a model / become

　→ _____

3 to her / apologize / is / what you should do

　→ _____

4 others / it / important / is / listen carefully to

　→ _____

C 보기의 동사를 이용하여 문장을 완성하시오.

보기	criticize	not/eat	help	meet

1 The reason I started volunteering is _____ _____ people in need.

2 One of my diet rules is _____ _____ _____ too much at once.

3 _____ _____ is easy, but to do is difficult.

4 We agreed _____ _____ on Friday, but he suddenly canceled.

D 주어진 두 문장을 to부정사를 이용하여 한 문장으로 쓰시오.

1 You ride a motorcycle without a helmet. That is dangerous.
→ It's dangerous _____.

2 You make a list before you make a big decision. That is useful.
→ It is _____.

3 You live by yourself. Isn't it lonely?
→ Isn't it _____?

WRITING PRACTICE

우리말과 일치하도록 「It ~ to-v」 구문과 괄호 안의 말을 이용하여 문장을 완성하시오.

1 그가 그 시험에서 부정행위를 했다는 것은 믿기 어렵다. (hard, believe, cheat on the test)

_____

2 고기보다는 채소를 사는 것이 더 쌌다. (cheaper, buy, vegetables, than, meat)

_____

3 당신의 실수들을 인정하지 않는 것은 잘못이다. (wrong, admit, mistakes)

_____

4 일본을 방문하기 위해 비자가 있을 필요는 없다. (necessary, have a visa, visit, Japan)

_____

UNIT 20 명사처럼 쓰이는 to부정사 II

⤵ **CHECK UP** 괄호 안에서 알맞은 것을 고르시오.

1 I planned (to read / reading) one book a week. 　A

2 My friends asked (me to have / to have me) a Christmas party. 　B

3 Would you know (what to do / to do what) if there was a fire in the building? 　D

4 I found (very difficult it / it very difficult) to find a good restaurant in this town. 　C

A 다음 상황에 맞게 빈칸에 알맞은 말을 써 넣으시오.

0 Sam : Shall we stop by a coffee shop?

Lisa : That sounds great.

→ They decided <u>to stop by</u> a coffee shop.

1 Jack : Could you help me?

Jane : Sure.

→ She agreed _____ him.

2 Mother : Pick up your clothes.

Ben : Okay.

→ She told him _____ his clothes.

3 Laura : Don't be late!

Peter : Don't worry. I won't.

→ She warned him _____.

B 보기에 주어진 말과 괄호 안의 의문사를 이용하여 문장을 완성하시오.

보기	install	eat	call	invite	operate

0 Please tell me <u>where to install</u> the air conditioner. (where)

1 I can't figure out _____ this machine. (how)

2 Have you decided _____ for lunch? (what)

3 She didn't tell me _____ her back. (when)

4 I don't know _____ to the party. (who)

C 다음 문장에서 어법상 <u>틀린</u> 곳을 찾아 고치시오. 틀린 곳이 없으면 O표 하시오.

1 They agreed sharing the cost of the taxi ride.

2 I found it very scary to have an operation.

3 Did you ever expect him buy you such an expensive ring?

D 주어진 문장과 같은 뜻이 되도록 빈칸을 채우시오.

0 My mother said I could stay up late.
→ My mother allowed <u>me to stay up late.</u>

1 Don't let me forget to pick up the kids from school.
→ Remind _____ .

2 My teacher said I should study computer programming.
→ My teacher encouraged _____ .

3 The doctor told me I should not eat salty food.
→ The doctor advised _____ .

WRITING PRACTICE

괄호 안의 말과 to부정사를 이용하여 영작을 완성하시오.

1 경비원이 너에게 어디로 갈지 알려줄 거야. (tell, go)

The security guard will _____ _____ _____ _____
_____ .

2 나는 그가 영어 공부를 하도록 설득하는 것이 힘들다는 것을 깨달았다. (it, difficult, persuade)

I found _____ _____ _____ _____
_____ study English.

3 네가 무언가에 대해 나를 도와줘야 해. (help)

I need _____ _____ _____ _____ with something.

4 문제는 언제 내 직장을 그만두느냐이다. (quit, my job)

The question is _____ _____ _____ _____ _____ .

정답 및 해설 p.32

UNIT 21 형용사처럼 쓰이는 to부정사

CHECK UP   괄호 안에서 알맞은 것을 고르시오.

1 I want to have a friend (to talk / to talk with).   `B-2`

2 The best way (to predict / predict) the future is to create it.   `A-1`

3 Juliet (never was to see / was never to see) Romeo again.   `C`

4 The aircraft appears (have crashed / to have crashed) near Kathmandu.   `A-2`

A   주어진 말을 알맞게 배열하여 문장을 완성하시오. (필요한 경우 to부정사를 이용할 것)

0 tell / you / an / interesting / story

→ I have <u>an interesting story to tell you.</u>

1 the first / on the Moon / walk / man

→ He was _____ .

2 go to the party / someone / with

→ He needs _____ .

3 go / the best / hiking / time

→ Spring is _____ .

B   보기에서 알맞은 것을 골라 「be to-v」 구문을 이용하여 빈칸을 채우시오.

보기	organize	turn	lose	succeed	wait

0 Patrick <u>is to organize</u> the presentation for tomorrow's meeting.

1 If you _____ in your work, you need to try harder.

2 They _____ for an hour before they finally got into the restaurant.

3 My father _____ 60 years old next year.

4 The team did their best, but they _____ in the final round.

C 다음 문장에서 어법상 틀린 곳을 찾아 고치시오. 틀린 곳이 없으면 O표 하시오.

1 This medicine is to be taken before meals.

2 Rachel, have you found a new apartment to live?

3 It's the most appropriate time making a new start.

4 We need a technician to fix the computers.

5 Joe didn't have anything else do, so he decided to go to bed.

D 괄호 안의 말을 알맞게 배열하여 문장을 완성하시오.

1 He is (an assistant, looking for, help with, to, his research).

2 She (to, return, never, again, home, was).

3 What (to, is, stress, the best way, relieve)?

4 The wedding reception (to, is, be, at the Windsor Hotel, hosted).

5 Darren (his promise, shopping, forgot about, go, to).

WRITING PRACTICE

괄호 안의 말을 이용하여 영작을 완성하시오.

1 나는 네게 가르칠 것이 아무것도 없다. (nothing, teach)

I _____ _____ _____ _____ you.

2 그 세미나는 이번 금요일에 열릴 예정이다. (be to, hold)

The seminar _____ _____ _____ _____ this Friday.

3 만약 쓸 펜이 필요하시면, 서랍 속을 한번 찾아보세요. (write)

If you need a pencil _____ _____ _____, take a look in the drawer.

4 그 소문은 거짓말로 판명되었다. (prove, a lie)

The rumor _____ _____ _____ _____ _____.

5 모든 질문에 답할 충분한 시간이 있을 것이다. (enough, answer)

You will have _____ _____ _____ _____ all the questions.

↗ **CHECK UP** 괄호 안에서 알맞은 것을 고르시오.

1 Bill hurried (not so as to / so as not to) be late for class again. B-1

2 I visited the Louvre Museum, (only to find / but to find) it closed. B-3

3 (Not to mention / To tell the truth), I'm afraid of her. C

4 Jack wore a suit (in order to / so that) make a better impression. B-2

A 주어진 두 문장을 「so that ~ can[could]」을 사용하여 한 문장으로 만드시오.

0 She ran. She wanted to catch the train.

→ She ran so that she could catch the train.

1 I sat in a window seat. I wanted to see the landscape.

→ _____

2 The woman interpreted for me. She wanted me to understand the speech.

→ _____

3 Please be on time. We want to depart before the weather gets bad.

→ _____

B 주어진 문장과 같은 뜻이 되도록 to부정사를 활용하여 빈칸을 채우시오.

1 I arrived and found that I was the first one there.

→ I arrived _____ _____ that I was the first one there.

2 He competed in the marathon but failed to finish.

→ He competed in the marathon, _____ _____

_____ to finish.

3 He left New York, and he never returned.

→ He left New York, _____ _____ _____.

4 If you saw him in person, you would never know he was a teacher.

→ _____ _____ _____ in person, you would

never know he was a teacher.

C 보기에서 가장 알맞은 말을 골라 빈칸에 쓰시오.

> 보기   strange to say   to make matters worse   not to mention

1 I had my cell phone stolen and _____, I lost my wallet.

2 Jane can speak Chinese, _____ English.

3 _____, no one has ever seen the writer in person.

D 밑줄 친 부분이 어법상 옳으면 O표 하고, 틀린 부분은 바르게 고치시오.

1 I <u>awoke find</u> it was still dark.

2 Anne wears skirts <u>in order look</u> feminine.

3 Oliver went to Beijing <u>to learn Chinese</u>.

4 <u>To hear his voice</u>, you would think he was a voice actor.

WRITING PRACTICE

괄호 안의 말과 to부정사를 이용하여 영작을 완성하시오.

1 나는 그를 따라잡기 위해서 빨리 걸어야만 했다. (walk fast)

I had to _____ _____ _____ keep up with him.

2 간단히 말해서 그는 해고되었다. (put)

_____ _____ _____ _____, he got fired.

3 Jennifer는 자라나서 유명한 요리사가 되었다. (grow up, become)

Jennifer _____ _____ _____ _____ a famous chef.

4 우리는 따뜻해지려고 불 가까이 다가갔다. (in order, get warm)

We moved closer to the fire _____ _____ _____ _____

_____.

5 Beth는 상사에게 좋은 인상을 주려고 대개 일찍 출근한다. (so as, impress)

Beth usually gets to work early _____ _____ _____ _____
the boss.

정답 및 해설 p.35

↗ **CHECK UP** 괄호 안에서 알맞은 것을 고르시오.

1 I'm really (happy to join / to happy join) this team. `A-1`

2 It was brave (for Jim / of Jim) to tell us the truth. `A-2`

3 Vera (was hesitant to / was hesitation to) ask him out. `Learn More Expressions`

4 This table is (too small / so small) for all of us (to sit / sit) around. `B-1`

5 He is (enough strong / strong enough) to lift the stone. `B-2`

A 주어진 문장과 같은 뜻이 되도록 빈칸을 채우시오.

0 It was silly of him to make such a mistake.

= He was <u>silly to make such a mistake</u>.

1 It is likely that the stormy weather will continue for three more days.

= The stormy weather _____.

2 The downtown area is impossible to reach in an hour.

= It is _____.

3 This road is so busy that children can't cross safely.

= This road is _____.

4 I'm sorry that I missed your birthday party.

= I'm sorry _____.

B 괄호 안의 말을 알맞게 배열하여 문장을 완성하시오.

1 It is (kind, me, to, give, a ride, of you) to work.

2 It was (leave, her bag, of her, to, careless) at work.

3 I (hear, was, to, delighted) that you're getting married.

4 He is always (somebody, ready, to, in need, help).

5 Barbara works so hard. She (to, be, is, certain, rich).

C 다음 문장에서 어법상 <u>틀린</u> 곳을 찾아 고치시오. 틀린 곳이 없으면 O표 하시오.

1 It's not easy to know how she's feeling.

2 The players are determined winning the competition.

3 You look tired too to play tennis with us.

4 My brother isn't enough old to ride the roller coaster.

D 주어진 두 문장을 too 또는 enough를 이용하여 한 문장으로 만드시오.

1 I arrived late. I couldn't catch the train.

→ _____

2 He was busy. He couldn't attend his daughter's graduation.

→ _____

3 Mike was strong. He could carry the box.

→ _____

WRITING PRACTICE

괄호 안의 말을 이용하여 영작을 완성하시오.

1 Jim의 글씨는 알아보기 힘들다. (hard, read)

Jim's handwriting _____.

2 그는 경험이 너무 없어서 팀을 이끌 수 없다. (too, inexperienced, lead)

He _____ a team.

3 Mark는 그 선반에 손이 닿을 정도로 키가 크다. (tall, enough, reach)

Mark _____ the shelf.

4 그 싸움을 막으려 했다니 Eric은 참 용감했다. (brave, try)

Eric _____ to stop the fight.

☑ **CHECK UP** 괄호 안에서 알맞은 것을 고르시오.

1 Jane told (her boyfriend not to smoke / for her boyfriend not to smoke). `A-1`

2 Dr. Lee's lectures are hard (for freshmen / freshmen) to understand. `A-2`

3 It's very considerate (for you / of you) to help me with my bags. `A-2`

4 Karen seems (that is on holiday / to be on holiday). `B-1`

A 다음 밑줄 친 부분의 의미상 주어를 찾아 쓰시오.

1 I have decided to stop eating sweet food. [   ]

2 The teacher advised the students to listen carefully. [   ]

3 It took a long time for me to realize I had to change my attitude. [   ]

4 She asked her friend to look after her puppy while she went on vacation. [   ]

5 It is rude of you to cut in while others are talking. [   ]

B 괄호 안의 형용사를 이용하여 문장을 완성하시오.

0 You keep on getting up late.

→ It is lazy of you to keep on getting up late. (lazy)

1 People read books all the time.

→ It _____ all the time. (necessary)

2 Greg helped us to remodel our apartment.

→ It _____ us to remodel our apartment. (kind)

3 Men watch a lot of sports on TV.

→ It _____ a lot of sports on TV. (normal)

4 You lent me this money.

→ It _____ me this money. (very generous)

C   다음 문장에서 어법상 틀린 곳을 찾아 고치시오. 틀린 곳이 없으면 O표 하시오.

1 Sometimes it can be hard to accept the truth.

2 The police officer warned for him not to speed.

3 It was foolish for him to act in such a childish way.

4 The class is designed of you to learn stress management techniques.

D   주어진 문장과 같은 뜻이 되도록 빈칸을 채우시오.

0 Max appears to be happy.

= It appears that Max is happy.

1 Kathy seemed to understand the problem.

= It seemed that _____.

2 It appears that they developed a similar style.

= They appear _____.

3 Justin seemed to have been given incorrect information.

= It seemed that _____.

4 It seems that he was careless in preparing for his test.

= He seems _____.

WRITING PRACTICE

괄호 안의 말을 이용하여 영작을 완성하시오.

1 네가 이사하는 것을 도와주다니 그는 친절했네. (kind, help)

It was _____ _____ _____ _____ you move
out.

2 Maria는 일전에 다친 것으로 보였었어. (appear, hurt)

Maria _____ _____ _____ _____ herself the other day.

3 Anne은 어제 자기 지갑을 잃어버렸던 것 같다. (seem, lose)

Anne _____ _____ _____ _____ her purse yesterday.

4 내 아버지는 내게 돈을 낭비하지 말라고 말씀하셨다. (tell, not, waste)

My father _____ _____ _____ _____ money.

⤢ **CHECK UP**   괄호 안에서 알맞은 것을 고르시오.

1 I heard someone (enter / to enter) the house.   `B`

2 He helped me (put / putting) my luggage on the scale.   `C-4`

3 Kate's outfit makes her (look / to look) older than she is.   `C-1`

4 Sue had her cell phone (repair / repaired) yesterday.   `C-2`

5 My mother got me (to open / open) the door.   `C-2`

A   괄호 안에 주어진 말을 빈칸에 알맞은 형태로 쓰시오.

1 He felt something _____ his back. (hit)

2 Mom said driving was dangerous and wouldn't let me _____ it. (do)

3 Dad got me _____ the garden this morning. (water)

4 The show was so funny. It made me _____. (laugh)

5 The police warned the protesters _____ special care. (take)

B   보기에서 알맞은 것을 골라 빈칸에 알맞은 형태로 쓰시오.

보기	talk	sign	lose	cut	share	dream

1 This movie made him _____ of becoming an actor.

2 I had my hair _____ yesterday.

3 I overheard them _____ about laying off people.

4 You must be hungry. Let me _____ my sandwich with you.

5 The argument caused her _____ her temper.

6 Did you see Brian _____ the document the other day?

C 다음 문장에서 어법상 <u>틀린</u> 곳을 찾아 고치시오. 틀린 곳이 없으면 O표 하시오.

1 What's in the box? Why won't you let me see it?

2 Jerry got his girlfriend drive him to the airport.

3 This exercise program will help strengthen your muscles.

4 I had my car fix last week.

5 The story I read on the Internet made me to cry.

D 자연스러운 대화가 되도록 괄호 안에서 알맞은 것을 고르시오.

1 A : Where is Noah?

B : I heard him (ask / asked / to ask) his teacher if he could leave early.

2 A : Is she having her knee (operate / operated / operating) on this Saturday?

B : No. It's next Saturday.

3 A : Did you see the show? That guy was hilarious.

B : Yes. I couldn't help (laugh / laughing / to laugh) out loud at his jokes.

WRITING PRACTICE

괄호 안의 말을 이용하여 영작을 완성하시오.

1 나는 그녀가 춤추는 것을 보았을 때, 그녀가 너무 우스워 보였다. (see, dance)

When I _____ _____ _____, she looked so funny.

2 너는 울타리를 페인트칠할 예정이니? (be going to, have, paint)

_____ you _____ _____ _____ the fence _____?

3 나는 갑자기 나의 얼굴이 붉어지는 것을 느꼈다. (feel, turn)

I suddenly _____ my face _____ _____.

4 우리 부모님은 나를 걱정하기만 하신다. (nothing, worry about)

My parents _____ _____ but _____ _____ _____.

5 이메일 청구서를 받음으로써 환경을 보호하는 것을 도와주세요. (help, protect)

_____ _____ the _____ by getting email bills.

UNIT 26 자주 쓰이는 to부정사 구문

↗ **CHECK UP** 괄호 안에서 알맞은 것을 고르시오.

1 She doesn't (seem to / happen to) be happy anymore.   `A`

2 The movie proved (being / to be) a great success.   `A`

3 Alice (advised / was advised) me not to go out with him.   `B`

4 Employees (do not allow / are not allowed) to smoke in the building.   `C`

A 다음 빈칸에 공통으로 들어갈 말을 보기에서 찾아 알맞은 형태로 쓰시오.

보기   manage to   fail to   tend to   try to

1 a. Never _____ lie to me again.

b. Did she ever _____ apologize and make up for it?

2 a. There _____ be jealousy when a new sibling comes along.

b. Written language _____ be more formal than spoken language.

3 a. I _____ get a table at the restaurant. All the tables were taken.

b. Thomas _____ get a promotion, and he complained about it.

4 a. I _____ get up early enough to take photos of the sunrise yesterday.

b. The airplane _____ land safely even though the weather was poor.

B 괄호 안에 주어진 말을 이용하여 빈칸을 완성하시오.

1 Bobby _____ drive his father's car yesterday. (allow)

2 Nowadays, many universities _____ their students _____ speak English. (require)

3 Russell _____ stop bothering his neighbors the other day. (tell)

4 The company _____ expand, but it decreased in size. (expect)

5 When she was a child, Emma's parents _____ her _____ become a surgeon. (encourage)

C 밑줄 친 부분이 어법상 옳으면 O표 하고, 틀린 부분은 바르게 고치시오.

1 Do you happen to know his address?

2 Doyle appears understanding the situation.

3 Sam was expected to come here.

4 The students asked the doorman let them in.

5 In order to pay off her debt, she forced to sell her precious jewels.

D 우리말과 일치하도록 괄호 안의 말을 알맞게 배열하시오.

1 좌석이 모두 찼지만, 나는 간신히 입석을 구할 수 있었다.

All the seats were taken, but (I, to, standing room, managed, find).

2 승객은 탑승 중에 휴대폰을 사용하는 것이 허용되지 않습니다.

(are, use, passengers, not, to, cell phones, permitted) on board.

3 Penny의 여동생은 Penny에게 함께 발리에 가자고 설득했다.

Her sister (go, to Bali, Penny, persuaded, to) with her.

WRITING PRACTICE

괄호 안의 말을 이용하여 영작을 완성하시오.

1 Jenny는 자신이 본 것을 과장하는 경향이 있어. (tend, exaggerate)

Jenny _____ what she sees.

2 나는 장학금으로 해외에서 공부를 할 수 있게 되었다. (enable, study)

A scholarship _____ abroad.

3 관광객들은 많은 돈을 가지고 다니지 말라는 충고를 들었다. (advise, not, carry)

The tourists _____ much money with them.

4 나쁜 날씨가 모든 항공편을 결항시켰다. (cause, all the flights, be)

The bad weather _____ canceled.

5 사람들은 정부에게 그 사고를 재조사하라고 촉구했다. (urge, the government, reinvestigate)

People _____ the accident.

UNIT 27 동명사의 개념 및 역할

정답 및 해설 p.40

↗ **CHECK UP** 괄호 안에서 알맞은 것을 고르시오.

1 She will never give up (auditioning / audition) for a role.　`B-3`

2 (Eat / Eating) slowly is one of the best ways to lose weight.　`B-1`

3 I'm really interested in (writing / write) stories.　`B-4`

4 I enjoy (not getting up / getting up not) early on the weekends.　`A`

A 보기에 주어진 말을 동명사로 바꾸어 빈칸에 쓰시오.

> 보기　go　　　learn　　　make　　　help　　　eat

1 _____ too much greasy food is bad for your heart.

2 I think _____ homeless people is good for society.

3 We talked about _____ to France for our vacation.

4 Bart apologized for _____ a mistake.

5 _____ to manage your time is important for your career.

B 괄호 안에 주어진 말을 빈칸에 알맞은 형태로 쓰시오.

1 It is not _____ an injury. (worth, risk)

2 I'm _____ to the opera this weekend. It's my first time.
(look forward to, go)

3 Jeanne _____ things online, doesn't she? (enjoy, buy)

4 My friends say I'm really _____ my teacher's voice.
(good at, mimic)

5 My wife _____ a vacation abroad. (insist on, take)

C 각 상황을 설명하는 문장을 동명사를 이용하여 완성하시오.

1 Jack: What shall we do?　　　　　Jill: We could go to the movies.
　→ Jill suggested _____.

---

2 Ann: You were driving too fast.   Dan: You're right. Sorry.

→ Dan admitted _____ .

3 Lily: You broke the laptop.   Sam: No, I didn't!

→ Sam denied _____ .

D   **주어진 문장과 같은 뜻이 되도록 동명사를 이용하여 빈칸을 채우시오.**

1 I will continue to help people in need.

= I won't stop _____ .

2 It can be good for your health to have a pet.

= _____ can be good for your health.

3 His main responsibility was to design security systems.

= _____ was his main responsibility.

4 There is a good chance that we will win the championship.

= We have a good chance of _____ .

5 He was afraid that he might hurt her feelings.

= He was afraid of _____ .

WRITING PRACTICE

괄호 안의 말을 이용하여 영작을 완성하시오.

1 나는 그의 변명을 듣는 데 질렸다. (tired of, hear)

I am _____ _____ _____ his excuses.

2 우리의 가장 큰 소망은 두 개의 한국을 통일하는 것이다. (unify, the two Koreas)

Our greatest hope is _____ _____ _____ _____ .

3 그는 지난달에 근처의 체육관에서 운동하기 시작했다. (start, work out)

He _____ _____ _____ at a nearby gym last month.

4 빵을 굽는 것은 당신이 생각하는 것보다 훨씬 쉽다. (bake bread)

_____ _____ is much easier than you might think.

⤴ **CHECK UP**   **괄호 안에서 알맞은 것을 고르시오.**

1 I clearly recall (his telling / telling his) the story.   `A-2`

2 Lily boasted of (being be / having been) the winner of the contest.   `B-2`

3 He was upset at (having insulted / having been insulted) in front of   `C-2`
his colleagues.

4 I worry about (he / him) driving at night.   `A-2`

A   **주어진 문장과 같은 뜻이 되도록 동명사를 이용하여 빈칸을 채우시오.**

1 Mr. Kim complained that we came to class late.

= Mr. Kim complained about _____ .

2 I want you to send it again.

= Would you mind _____ ?

3 We all expect Mary to come back for Christmas.

= We're all looking forward to _____ .

4 He admitted that he had lost the tickets for the musical.

= He admitted _____ .

5 Paula is ashamed that she spoke so rudely.

= Paula is ashamed of _____ .

B   **보기에 주어진 말을 동명사의 능동형 또는 수동형으로 바꾸어 빈칸에 쓰시오.**

보기   organize   open   laugh at   treat

1 Do you mind _____ the window for me?

2 Nobody likes _____ by other people.

3 Have you started _____ your schedule?

4 Puppies love _____ with affection.

C 괄호 안의 명사 또는 대명사를 동명사의 의미상 주어로 하여 문장을 완성하시오.

1 I had no doubts about passing the exam. (you)

→ I had no doubts about _____.

2 He's worried about playing mobile games too much. (she)

→ He's worried about _____.

3 Jake was proud of having been selected as a finalist. (his daughter)

→ Jake was proud of _____.

D 괄호 안의 말을 이용하여 영작을 완성하시오.

1 나는 그가 늦는 것을 이해할 수 없다. (understand, be late)

I don't _____ _____ _____.

2 그는 아무런 이유 없이 벌을 받았던 것 때문에 화가 났다. (upset, punish)

He _____ _____ due to _____

_____ _____ for no reason.

3 나는 그가 Jenny를 선택한 것에 놀랐다. (choose)

I was surprised at _____ _____ Jenny.

WRITING PRACTICE

우리말과 일치하도록 괄호 안의 말을 알맞게 배열하시오.

1 우리는 그 여배우가 여우주연상을 받은 것에 기뻐했다. (been, with, having, the actress, given)

We were pleased _____ the Best Actress award.

2 그 상황이 내가 마감을 지키지 못하는 결과를 낳았다. (missing, the deadline, my)

The circumstances resulted in _____.

3 의장은 그 회의가 지연된 것에 대해 사과했다. (having, for, delayed, the meeting, been)

The chairman apologized _____.

4 사랑에 빠진다는 것은 마법 구름에 사로잡히는 것과 같다. (like, being, in, wrapped, a magical cloud)

Falling in love is _____.

UNIT 29 동명사 vs. to부정사

☑ **CHECK UP** 괄호 안에서 알맞은 것을 고르시오.

1 Finally, I can afford (to buy / buying) a car. `A`

2 Nell refused (to help / helping) clean the house. `A`

3 Keep (to go / going) until you come to a department store. `A`

4 I regret not (to study / studying) harder. `C`

5 She denied ever (to have met / having met) the man. `A`

A 보기에 주어진 말을 동명사 또는 to부정사로 바꾸어 빈칸에 쓰시오.

보기	go	stay	clean	introduce	eat	become

1 I try to avoid _____ unhealthy food.

2 Jeff promised _____ me to a nice guy.

3 I prefer _____ home to going out.

4 Anita didn't expect _____ famous so quickly.

5 Shall we put off _____ the house until next weekend?

6 I wanted to go to Hawaii, but Ron suggested _____ to Monaco.

B 주어진 두 문장을 동명사 또는 to부정사를 이용하여 한 문장으로 만드시오.

0 Trevor didn't ring Laura. He forgot.

→ Trevor forgot to ring Laura.

1 They didn't advertise their products. Now they regret it.

→ They regret _____.

2 Mindy once visited Rome. She'll never forget it.

→ Mindy will never forget _____.

3 Mark's sister wanted him to call her back. He remembered it.

→ Mark remembered _____.

C 다음 문장에서 어법상 <u>틀린</u> 곳을 찾아 고치시오. 틀린 곳이 없으면 O표 하시오.

1 I agreed going to the opera.

2 If you stop to practice, you'll never get better.

3 The company expects to hiring hundreds of workers this year.

4 Though she tried taking some aspirin, the pain didn't go away.

D 괄호 안의 말을 알맞게 배열하여 문장을 완성하시오. (동사의 시제와 형태를 알맞게 변형할 것)

1 Owen (always, lock, remember, the door) before leaving.

2 I will (Mt. Everest, never, climb, for the first time, forget).

3 When traveling, I (prefer, to, take, drive) a train.

4 I now (not, my brother's advice, listen to, regret). He was right.

5 Ross (gasoline, stop, yesterday, get) and was shocked at the price.

WRITING PRACTICE

괄호 안의 말을 이용하여 영작을 완성하시오.

1 몇몇 대기업들이 자주 지급을 연기한다. (delay, pay, their bills)

Some big companies often _____ _____ _____ _____.

2 몇 달 만에 외국어를 배울 수 있다는 기대는 하지 말아라. (expect, a foreign language)

Don't _____ _____ _____ _____ _____
_____ in a few months.

3 나는 여전히 내 첫차를 산 것을 기억한다. (remember)

I still _____ _____ _____ _____ _____.

4 저는 귀사에서 근무하기를 희망합니다. (hope, work for)

I _____ _____ _____ _____ your company.

UNIT 30 자주 쓰이는 동명사 구문

정답 및 해설 p.44

CHECK UP 괄호 안에서 알맞은 것을 고르시오.

1 I can't help but (smile / to smile) when I look at my kids.   `a`

2 Sarah used to (work / working) in a theater in her 20s.   `e`

3 This film is worth (to see / seeing).   `h`

4 I don't feel like (eating / to eat) out tonight.   `i`

5 A traffic jam kept me from (arrive / arriving) at the airport on time.   `k`

A

밑줄 친 동사를 어법에 맞게 고쳐 쓰시오.

1 I couldn't help <u>drop</u> the hot plate.

2 It is no use <u>regret</u> what is done.

3 Never work out without <u>stretch</u> first.

4 She tried to stop her son from <u>spend</u> hours at the computer, but failed.

5 My family is accustomed to my <u>come</u> home late.

6 There is no <u>succeed</u> without a lot of hard work.

B

주어진 문장과 같은 뜻이 되도록 동명사를 이용하여 빈칸을 채우시오.

1 As soon as I saw Ronald, I knew he had bad news.

= _____ Ronald, I knew he had bad news.

2 He was about to speak when the phone rang.

= He was on the point of _____.

3 It is useless to try to explain things to a dog.

= It is no _____ to a dog.

4 Emma couldn't help but disobey the order.

= Emma couldn't _____.

70 G-ZONE WORKBOOK

C 다음 문장에서 어법상 <u>틀린</u> 곳을 찾아 고치시오. 틀린 곳이 없으면 O표 하시오.

1 Her child is used to walk by himself now.

2 I'm looking forward to my boyfriend's Christmas present.

3 I spent years try to learn how to speak Chinese.

4 Olive was on the point of cry when I tried to talk to her.

D 보기에 주어진 말과 괄호 안의 동사를 이용하여 문장을 완성하시오.

보기   be accustomed to   keep/from   be busy   have trouble   feel like

1 I think she is rude. I don't _____ to her ever again. (talk)

2 Worries _____ him _____ properly last night. (sleep)

3 I always seem to _____ files to you. It never works. (send)

4 I can't go with you. I _____ the laundry right now. (do)

5 I've worked in customer service for years, so I _____ rude people. (deal with)

WRITING PRACTICE

괄호 안의 말을 이용하여 영작을 완성하시오.

1 그들은 만나기만 하면 싸운다. (never, fight)

They _____ meet _____ _____.

2 폭설이 와서 Peter는 파티에 가지 못했다. (prevent, go)

Heavy snow _____ Peter _____ _____ _____ the party.

3 어제 나는 그녀에게 새집을 찾아주는 데 어려움을 겪었다. (have, difficulty, find)

Yesterday, I _____ _____ _____ _____ a new house.

4 그가 중국어를 매우 잘 한다는 것은 말할 필요도 없다. (go, say, speak)

It _____ _____ _____ that _____ can _____ Chinese very well.

1 다음 중 어법상 맞는 것을 고르시오.

① Is that easy to solve this problem?
② I can't help to fall in love with you.
③ They agreed continuing the discussion.
④ My mom doesn't allow me watching TV.
⑤ The prisoners complained of having been treated harshly.

2 다음 중 의미가 <u>다른</u> 하나를 고르시오.

① She ran fast to catch the train.
② She ran fast in order to catch the train.
③ She ran fast so that she could catch the train.
④ She ran fast so as to catch the train.
⑤ She ran so fast that she could catch the train.

3 두 문장이 같은 의미가 되도록 괄호 안의 말을 이용하여 빈칸을 채우시오.

He was so smart that he was able to graduate from high school early. (enough)
→ He was _____ _____ _____ _____ from high school early.

4 (A), (B), (C) 각각에 들어갈 단어를 쓰시오.

(A) It's very nice _____ you to show me the way.
(B) It was hard _____ me to pass the exam.
(C) It's foolish _____ you to tell a lie.

5 밑줄 친 부분이 어법상 <u>틀린</u> 것을 고르시오.

James was a good English teacher. ① <u>Teaching</u> English was fun for him, and his students enjoyed ② <u>taking</u> his class. When his wife was diagnosed with cancer in 2015, however, he decided ③ <u>to stop</u> teaching. He wanted ④ <u>taking</u> care of his wife instead. He is not a teacher anymore, but he is still proud of ⑤ <u>having been</u> a teacher.

6 다음 중 어법상 틀린 것을 <u>모두</u> 고르시오.

① It was difficult to use the machine.
② Is there anything eat in the refrigerator?
③ He tried to forget the car accident.
④ Why don't we go out instead of watching TV?
⑤ He didn't admit to cheat on the exam.

7 다음을 읽고, 같은 의미가 되도록 빈칸에 알맞은 말을 쓰시오.

> David made fun of Sue in front of their classmates, so she is angry at him. Now he regrets what he did.

→ David regrets _____ _____
_____ Sue.

8 밑줄 친 부분이 어법상 틀린 것을 고르시오.

> I ① used to live in the country. I enjoyed playing outside with my friends and ② growing vegetables in the garden. When I moved to the city, I ③ wasn't accustomed to take the subway. Also, the air wasn't ④ as clean as it was in the country. However, I soon ⑤ got used to living there.

9 다음 대화문 중 어색한 것을 고르시오.

① A : Have you finished your homework?
   B : Not yet. I have a lot to do.
② A : What should I do to become a better student?
   B : Just do what you're supposed to do.
③ A : Would you mind to take our picture?
   B : Sure. Which button should I press?
④ A : When did you get your hair cut?
   B : Yesterday. Do you like it?
⑤ A : My brother is mean. I don't know what to do.
   B : Tell your mom about his behavior.

[10-11] 우리말과 일치하도록 괄호 안의 말을 바르게 배열하시오.

10
> 그들은 금요일까지 과제를 제출해야 한다.
> (are, hand in, to, their reports)

→ They _____
_____ by Friday.

11
> 그는 지갑을 훔친 것으로 의심받았다.
> (of, a purse, stolen, having)

→ He was suspected _____
_____.

12 빈칸에 들어갈 수 없는 것을 고르시오.

> He never _____ going out with her.

① considered   ② admitted
③ enjoyed   ④ planned
⑤ felt like

13 다음 중 밑줄 친 부분의 쓰임이 바른 것을 고르시오.

① I'm looking forward to see you again.
② They were opposed to selling the family business.
③ I was encouraged to saving half of my allowance.
④ I'm having trouble to sleep recently.
⑤ Students are not allowed to drinking alcohol.

14 어법상 <u>틀린</u> 곳을 찾아 고치시오. (2개)

> Summer is coming. I will go fishing and swimming every day, and sleep until noon. I'll be busy to ride my bike and watch movies. I won't have to worry about getting my homework done or failing a test.

15 두 문장의 의미가 <u>다른</u> 것을 고르시오.

① She was on the point of opening the door.
  → She was about to open the door.
② I don't feel like going to the party.
  → I don't want to go to the party.
③ On arriving in Seoul, he called me.
  → Before he arrived in Seoul, he called me.
④ Bad weather kept us from traveling.
  → We couldn't travel due to bad weather.
⑤ It is no use arguing with him.
  → It is useless to argue with him.

16 빈칸에 알맞은 것을 고르시오.

> This article will be easy _____ to translate.

① for you
② of you
③ with you
④ your
⑤ yours

17 두 문장이 같은 의미가 되도록 빈칸에 알맞은 말을 쓰시오.

> It seems that she was a flight attendant.
> → She seems _____ _____ _____ a flight attendant.

18 빈칸에 공통으로 들어갈 단어를 쓰시오.

> (A) I found _____ impossible to keep silent about what had happened to me.
> (B) _____ is believed that children learn foreign languages very quickly.

19 우리말과 일치하도록 괄호 안의 말을 활용하여 문장을 완성하시오.

> 약이 너무 써서 내가 삼킬 수 없었다. (bitter, swallow)

→ The medicine was _____
_____.

20 밑줄 친 부분의 의미상 주어가 <u>다른</u> 하나를 고르시오.

> Dad insisted on my ① going to Oxford University, but I didn't want ② to go there. The only reason for him ③ to push me was that he graduated from Oxford. He finally persuaded me ④ to apply to the university by taking me there for a visit. I loved it! I've decided ⑤ to major in art history.

21 다음 중 어법상 틀린 것을 고르시오.

① I think his novel is worth reading.
② Yoga helps me relieve stress.
③ Watching TV makes me feel better.
④ It's nice to hear Jane to play the piano.
⑤ I had my eyes tested at an eye clinic.

22 [보기]의 to visit과 쓰임이 같은 것을 고르시오.

> **[보기]** When is the best time to visit Taiwan?

① She awoke to find herself famous.
② He must be a fool to do such a thing.
③ It is impossible for him to multitask.
④ Her job is to analyze evidence from the crime scene.
⑤ We're looking for volunteers to take care of abandoned animals.

[23-24] 다음 글을 읽고, 물음에 답하시오.

Dorothy ① sat down on the grass and looked at her companions, and they sat down and looked at her. Toto found ② that for the first time in his life he was too tired ⓐ (chase) a butterfly that flew ③ past his head. So he ④ puts out his tongue and panted, looking at Dorothy ⑤ with great fatigue.

23 ①~⑤ 중에서 어법상 틀린 것을 고르시오.

①   ②   ③   ④   ⑤

24 괄호 ⓐ 안의 (chase)를 어법에 맞게 쓰시오.

[25-26] 다음 글을 읽고, 물음에 답하시오.

If you spend some time ① to talk with CeCe Winans, a well-known singer, you ② will find that she is a confident, successful woman. However, she's also a working mom who puts her family before her work. Although she is proud of what women have achieved in music, sports, and business, she thinks ③ being a supportive wife and mother is also important. She is trying ④ to be a good example to her daughter as a woman who dedicates herself to her family. She says, "I ⑤ want my daughter to see that she can be a mom, she can have a family, and she can do what she loves to do."

25 ①~⑤ 중에서 어법상 틀린 것을 고르시오.

①   ②   ③   ④   ⑤

26 CeCe Winans에 대한 위 글의 내용과 일치하지 않는 것을 고르시오.

① 성공한 가수이다.
② 자신의 일보다 가족을 우선시하려고 노력한다.
③ 각 분야에서 여성들의 업적을 자랑스러워 한다.
④ 여성에게 가장 중요한 것은 아내로서의 역할이라고 생각한다.
⑤ 자신의 딸에게 모범이 되고 싶어 한다.

↗ CHECK UP   괄호 안에서 알맞은 것을 고르시오.

1 Do you know the girl (crying / cried) over there?   `A`

2 Jean was (exciting / excited) to go to the party.   `B-4`

3 I really want to eat a (baking / baked) potato.   `B-1`

4 He ate a bag of popcorn (watch / watching) the movie.   `B-3`

5 He found the coat (damaging / damaged).   `B-2`

A   괄호 안에 주어진 말을 빈칸에 알맞은 형태로 쓰시오.

1 The gifts _____ by Pat were really nice. (give)

2 I was disturbed by a _____ dog. (bark)

3 I noticed the old man _____ at me. (stare)

4 Have you heard of a movie _____ *Titanic*? (call)

5 He tried to open the _____ door, but he failed. (lock)

B   주어진 두 문장을 한 문장으로 만드시오.

0 I helped a woman. She was hurt in the accident.

  → I helped a woman <u>hurt in the accident</u>.

1 I saw a girl. She was chasing her dog.

  → I saw a girl _____.

2 The travel agency sent me a brochure. The brochure contained all the information I needed.

  → The travel agency sent me a brochure _____.

3 I think the man is innocent. He is suspected of being a robber.

  → I think the man _____ is innocent.

C 다음 문장에서 어법상 틀린 곳을 찾아 고치시오. 틀린 곳이 없으면 O표 하시오.

1 Most of the goods making in this factory are exported.

2 There were birds fly around our heads.

3 Maurice saw Joe dancing at the concert.

4 The dog frightening by the thunder hid under the table.

D 다음 밑줄 친 부분이 현재분사이면 '분', 동명사이면 '동'을 쓰시오.

1 Amanda is <u>focusing</u> on her career these days.　　　[　　]

2 All campers should bring their own <u>camping</u> gear.　　　[　　]

3 The <u>protesting</u> students marched through the city center.　[　　]

4 Her job is <u>overseeing</u> construction projects.　　　[　　]

5 I heard someone <u>playing</u> the violin.　　　[　　]

WRITING PRACTICE

괄호 안의 말을 이용하여 영작을 완성하시오.

1 잠자는 아기를 깨우지 않도록 해. (sleep, baby)

Do not wake up the ＿＿＿＿＿＿ ＿＿＿＿＿＿.

2 나는 두 개의 고장 난 카메라가 있어. 고쳐 줄 수 있니? (break, camera)

I have ＿＿＿＿＿＿ ＿＿＿＿＿＿ ＿＿＿＿＿. Can you fix them?

3 당신을 기다리는 택시가 있습니다. (wait)

There is ＿＿＿＿＿ ＿＿＿＿＿＿ ＿＿＿＿＿ for you.

4 그는 거칠게 소리지르면서 내 방 안으로 걸어 들어왔다. (walk into, shout)

He ＿＿＿＿＿ ＿＿＿＿＿＿ ＿＿＿＿＿ ＿＿＿＿＿ ＿＿＿＿＿ wildly.

5 그녀는 자기 아들이 바닥에서 장난감을 가지고 노는 모습을 지켜보았다. (watch, play)

She ＿＿＿＿＿ ＿＿＿＿＿＿ ＿＿＿＿＿ ＿＿＿＿＿ on the floor with his toy.

UNIT 32 능동의 v-ing vs. 수동의 v-ed

정답 및 해설 p.49

☑ **CHECK UP**   괄호 안에서 알맞은 것을 고르시오.

1 Bill had his hair (cut / cutting). `B-2`

2 She didn't say anything. She must have been (shocked / shocking) at the photo. `A-2`

3 I'm sorry to keep you (waiting / waited) for so long. `B-1`

4 I saw someone (breaking / broken) the kitchen windows. `B-2`

5 The company's sales for this year were (disappointing / disappointed). `A-1`

A   괄호 안에 주어진 말을 빈칸에 알맞은 형태로 쓰시오.

1 Serena went to see the musical. The performance was good. (satisfy)

　 a. The musical performance was _____.

　 b. Serena was _____ with the musical.

2 Those companies keep on phoning me. It really bothers me. (annoy)

　 a. Those companies are really _____.

　 b. Those companies make me _____.

　 c. It's pointless to get _____ because of those companies.

3 Karl is going to China on vacation. He has never been abroad. (interest)

　 a. It will be an _____ vacation for him.

　 b. Going on vacation is always _____.

　 c. Karl is really _____ in going to China.

B   괄호 안에 주어진 동사와 보기의 표현을 이용하여 문장을 완성하시오. (분사를 이용할 것)

보기	come to class	might lose	had walked

1 Doris seemed _____ that she _____ her savings. (worry)

2 She was _____ after she _____ 10 miles. (exhaust)

3 As a teacher, it's _____ when students _____ late. (irritate)

C 보기1과 보기2에서 표현을 골라 알맞은 형태로 바꾸어 문장을 완성하시오.

보기1	her shoulder	a thief	보기2	grab	play
	his song	her portrait		paint	run away

0 She felt <u>her shoulder grabbed</u> by someone.

1 The boy saw _____ from the police.

2 The woman had _____ by a famous artist.

3 The musician heard _____ on the radio.

D 다음 문장에서 어법상 틀린 곳을 찾아 고치시오. 틀린 곳이 없으면 O표 하시오.

1 We had our house remodeled.

2 It was an amazed play. Everybody was fascinated.

3 I saw him walked along the road.

4 The king had him throwing in prison.

WRITING PRACTICE

괄호 안의 말을 이용하여 영작을 완성하시오.

1 나는 그의 갑작스러운 방문에 놀랐다. (surprise)

_____ _____ _____ by his unexpected visit.

2 그의 강의가 지겨워서 나는 하품을 참을 수가 없었다. (his lecture, bore)

_____ _____ _____ , so I couldn't help yawning.

3 너는 지갑을 도둑맞은 적이 있니? (have, your wallet, steal)

Have you ever _____ _____ _____ _____ ?

4 그녀가 떠나려고 했을 때, 그녀는 자신이 방에 갇힌 것을 알았다. (find, herself, lock)

When she tried to leave, she _____ _____ _____ in the room.

5 개봉한 후에 이 소스는 냉장 보관되도록 해야 한다. (keep, this sauce, refrigerate)

You should _____ _____ _____ _____ once it is opened.

UNIT 33 분사구문

정답 및 해설 p.51

☑ **CHECK UP** 괄호 안에서 알맞은 것을 고르시오.

1 She watched TV all day long, (eating / eaten) ice cream and popcorn. `B-2`

2 (Tiring / Tired) of doing the same things every day, he quit his job. `B-4`

3 (Buy / Buying) the tickets, Tom went into the theater. `B-3`

4 (Not knowing / Knowing not) where to go, I asked a police officer. `A`

A 다음 밑줄 친 부분을 분사구문 또는 절로 바꾸시오.

1 <u>As I had no time</u>, I decided not to meet them.

→ _____, I decided not to meet them.

2 <u>If you turn left at the corner</u>, you will find the mall.

→ _____, you will find the mall.

3 <u>Waking up</u>, I discovered that everybody had already left.

→ _____, I discovered that everybody had already left.

4 I finished my homework <u>while I was listening to music</u>.

→ I finished my homework _____.

5 <u>Presented in Chinese</u>, the lecture was not easy to understand.

→ _____, it was not easy to understand.

6 <u>They said goodbye to their families</u> and got on the airplane.

→ _____, they got on the airplane.

7 She discovered many interesting places <u>while she was traveling around Asia</u>.

→ She discovered many interesting places _____.

8 <u>Leaving your house early</u>, you will avoid all the traffic.

→ _____, you will avoid all the traffic.

80 G-ZONE WORKBOOK

B 다음 문장에서 어법상 틀린 곳을 찾아 고치시오. 틀린 곳이 없으면 O표 하시오.

1 Writing in Latin, the text was hard to translate.

2 Driving home, I witnessed an accident.

3 Tried not to wake up others, she made breakfast in the kitchen.

4 Exhausted from so much exercise, she took a rest.

5 Wearing not a suit, I couldn't get into the restaurant.

C 보기에 주어진 부사절을 알맞은 분사구문으로 전환하여 문장을 완성하시오.

보기	when he opened a can	because he didn't feel well
	as he is a vegetarian	if he leaves now

0 Dave cut his finger opening a can.

1 _____, Nate came in late this morning.

2 _____, he can still catch the train.

3 _____, my brother doesn't eat any kind of meat.

WRITING PRACTICE

우리말과 일치하도록 괄호 안의 말을 이용하여 분사구문을 완성하시오.

1 무엇을 해야 할지 몰라서 나는 형에게 도움을 청했다. (know, what to do)

_____, I asked my brother for help.

2 그는 손가락으로 그의 눈을 문지르면서 침대에서 일어났다. (rub, with his fingers)

He got up from his bed _____.

3 그 파티를 준비하는 동안 그들은 엉망으로 만들었다. (prepare for)

_____, they made a mess.

4 그녀는 Tom을 방문해서 그에게 생일 선물을 주었다. (give, a birthday present)

She visited Tom, _____.

5 그녀의 지시를 따르면 너는 이 기술을 완전히 익힐 수 있을 것이다. (follow, instructions)

_____, you will be able to master this technique.

☑ **CHECK UP** 괄호 안에서 알맞은 것을 고르시오.

1 The presentation will be given today, (permitting time / time permitting). `B-1`

2 (Having seen / Seeing) the movie before, we decided to see another one. `A-1`

3 (Made of / Making of) plastic, it floats on the water. `A-2`

4 (Strictly speaking / Speaking of), this answer is wrong. `D`

5 She sat with her legs (crossing / crossed). `C`

A 다음 밑줄 친 부분을 분사구문으로 바꾸시오.

1 <u>After I had eaten dinner</u>, I fell asleep.

→ _____, I fell asleep.

2 <u>As she was delayed at the airport</u>, she couldn't make it to the wedding.

→ _____, she couldn't make it to the wedding.

3 <u>As it was late</u>, he stopped studying.

→ _____, he stopped studying.

4 <u>As the party had ended</u>, we went home.

→ _____, we went home.

B 보기에서 알맞은 말을 골라 빈칸에 쓰시오.

보기 frankly speaking   judging from   granted that   speaking of

1 _____ the way she speaks, she must be well educated.

2 _____, I think you should tell him you are sorry.

3 _____ I probably won't win, I'd still like to enter the competition.

4 _____ travel, I really want to visit Cambodia.

C 다음 문장에서 어법상 **틀린** 곳을 찾아 고치시오. 틀린 곳이 없으면 O표 하시오.

1 Having asked to keep it secret, I didn't tell anyone about her problem.

2 Generally speaking, men are better at finding their way than women.

3 It being cold, we decided to make a fire.

4 They were waiting outside with their arms folding.

D 괄호 안의 말을 알맞게 배열하여 문장을 완성하시오.

1 (finished, the, having, report) yesterday, I can go to the party tonight.

2 I couldn't concentrate (the, up, with, turned, sound).

3 (his, encouraging, mother, him), he moved to Los Angeles to pursue acting.

4 (in my garden, no, there, flowers, being), I decided to plant some.

5 (been, invited, to the party, having), I could hardly refuse to go.

6 (her, after, book, completed, having), she took a vacation.

WRITING PRACTICE

괄호 안의 말을 이용하여 영작을 완성하시오.

1 Jane은 불을 켜 놓은 채 잠이 들었다. (the light, turn on)

Jane fell asleep _____ _____ _____ _____.

2 그녀의 편지로 판단하건대, 그녀는 잘 지내는 것처럼 보인다. (judging from)

_____ _____ _____ _____, she seems to be fine.

3 날씨가 좋다면 우리는 캠핑을 갈 수 있다. (the weather, be, fine)

_____ _____ _____ _____, we can go camping.

4 유죄로 판명되어, 그는 벌금을 내도록 명령 받았다. (find, guilty)

_____ _____, he was ordered to pay a fine.

5 대학을 졸업하고, 그는 영화 제작자가 되었다. (have, graduate from, university)

_____ _____ _____ _____, he became a filmmaker.

↗ **CHECK UP** 괄호 안에서 알맞은 것을 고르시오.

1 He didn't speak to anyone, (and / but) nobody spoke to him.   B - 1

2 She can play both the piano (and / or) the guitar.   B - 1

3 My teacher gave me neither compliment (nor / or) punishment.   B - 3

4 I forgot his name suddenly, (or / so) I just smiled at him.   B - 4

5 Please fasten your seat belt, (and / or) you could get hurt.   B - 3

A 다음 a와 b의 문장을 box 안의 알맞은 접속사를 이용하여 연결하시오.

a

1 I bought a gift for her

2 Jenny was feeling hungry

3 I climbed to the top of the mountain

4 I wanted to say hello to him

5 Do you want to join us

| so |
| and |
| but |
| or |

b

a. I couldn't remember his name.

b. will you stay at home?

c. I forgot to give it to her.

d. she made herself a sandwich.

e. I looked at the view.

B 주어진 두 문장을 괄호 안의 접속사를 이용하여 한 문장으로 만드시오.

1 Greg wants to be a lawyer, or he wants to be an accountant.

→ Greg wants to be _____. (either ~ or)

2 The guidebook was not helpful. The maps were not helpful, either.

→ _____ helpful. (neither ~ nor)

3 George visited Rome. He also visited Athens.

→ George visited _____. (not only ~ but also)

→ George visited _____. (as well as)

C 다음 문장에서 어법상 **틀린** 곳을 찾아 고치시오. 틀린 곳이 없으면 O표 하시오.

1 He came home early not to help his wife but to watch the soccer game.

2 I'm interested only in painting but also in sculpture.

3 I usually don't drink, and I had some wine last night.

4 Larry must choose either to stay home or going out.

D 보기에서 알맞은 것을 골라 빈칸에 쓰시오.

보기	both	but	either	neither

1 I met _____ your sister or your cousin. I'm not sure which one.

2 _____ the kitchen and the living room need to be cleaned.

3 It is not only fun _____ also inspirational to travel abroad.

4 She is a vegetarian; she eats _____ meat nor fish.

WRITING PRACTICE

괄호 안의 말을 이용하여 영작을 완성하시오.

1 곧장 두 블록 가세요. 그러면 그 표지판을 볼 것입니다. (see, the sign)

Go straight for two blocks, _____ you _____ _____ _____
_____.

2 그것은 골동품이 아니라 모조품이다. (an antique, an imitation)

It is _____ _____ _____ _____ _____
_____.

3 택시나 전철을 타시면 됩니다. (a taxi, the subway)

You can take _____ _____ _____ _____
_____.

4 나는 그 문제를 상사에게 가져갔지만, 그는 그냥 그것을 웃어넘겼다. (just, laugh it off)

I brought the issue to my boss, _____ _____ _____ _____
_____ _____.

☑ **CHECK UP** 괄호 안에서 알맞은 것을 고르시오.

1 I absolutely agree with your idea (that / if) we need more trees. `B-1`

2 Do you know which car (will he / he will) choose? `C-1`

3 (Whether / That) you go there or not doesn't matter. `B-2`

4 (What do you believe / Do you believe what) is the best way? `C-1`

5 I just want to know (if / because) he is happy or not. `B-2`

A 빈칸에 that, whether 또는 if 중 알맞은 것을 쓰시오.

1 It seems _____ I am the only person who knows the truth.

2 I don't know _____ it's good to invite her or not.

3 It's great _____ you have found another job already.

4 I'm not sure of _____ he is guilty or not.

5 It's so fantastic _____ you've decided to come home for Christmas.

B 주어진 두 문장을 한 문장으로 만드시오.

1 I don't know. + How much does it cost?

→ _____

2 I wonder. + Is she going to marry him?

→ _____

3 Do you know? + Where is the subway station?

→ _____

4 Do you think? + What will she wear for the party?

→ _____

C 다음 문장에서 어법상 <u>틀린</u> 곳을 찾아 고치시오. 틀린 곳이 없으면 O표 하시오.

1 Can you show me how can I get there?

2 Whether you succeed or fail depends on many factors.

3 I forgot where I first met him.

4 Do you suppose how long it will take to get there?

D 보기에서 가장 알맞은 접속사를 골라 빈칸에 쓰시오.

보기	that	if	what	when

1 I asked her _____ she was Pete's sister.

2 Do you know _____ they will arrive at the airport? They didn't tell me the time.

3 She decided _____ she would not tell the truth to her parents.

4 _____ do you think is the best way to master Chinese?

WRITING PRACTICE

괄호 안의 말을 이용하여 영작을 완성하시오.

1 너는 이 방의 용도가 무엇일 것 같니? (think, this room)

_____ _____ you _____ _____ _____ is for?

2 그렇다고 해서 네가 그것을 내일까지 마쳐야 한다는 사실이 변하지는 않는다. (must, finish)

That does not change the fact _____ _____ _____ _____ it by tomorrow.

3 저는 이 자전거를 환불 받을 수 있는지 알고 싶어요. (get a refund)

I'd like to know _____ I can _____ _____ _____ for this bike.

4 문제는 정부가 우리의 개인 데이터에 대한 접근 권한을 가져야 하느냐이다. (the government, should, have access)

The question is _____ _____ _____ _____ _____ _____ to our personal data.

UNIT **37** 부사절 종속접속사 I (when, while, as, since, until, because ...)

정답 및 해설 p.56

☑ **CHECK UP** 괄호 안에서 알맞은 것을 고르시오.

1 (Until / As soon as) it got dark, I turned on the lights. `A-4`

2 I have played the piano (since / while) I was five. `A-5`

3 The music made me nervous (because / because of) the high-pitched sound. `B-1`

4 (That / Now that) the exam is over, I can focus on writing. `B-3`

5 I'll call you when (I will get / I get) there. `A-2`

A 보기에서 가장 알맞은 접속사를 골라 빈칸에 쓰시오. (단, 한 번씩만 쓸 것)

보기 since   as   until   because

1 I have been using this library _____ I was a child.

2 Let's wait here _____ the others arrive.

3 I couldn't go to the wedding _____ I was in Vancouver at the time.

4 _____ he grew older, he became quieter.

B 다음 빈칸에 공통으로 들어갈 접속사를 쓰시오.

1 a. _____ I am tired, I will go to bed.

b. _____ he made the sandwiches, I prepared the soup.

c. _____ soon _____ I graduate from college, I'm going to take a vacation.

2 a. I've had a terrible cold _____ last week.

b. Ever _____ I met you, you have been teasing me.

c. _____ you are the only person who speaks English, you should ask him.

3 a. He listens to music _____ he works.

b. _____ I enjoy watching baseball, I'm not into playing it.

c. I talked on the phone _____ I was walking home last night.

C 다음 문장에서 어법상 **틀린** 곳을 찾아 고치시오. 틀린 곳이 없으면 O표 하시오.

1 I'm interested in classical music because its depth.

2 Since it was snowing, we stayed indoors.

3 I will visit the Eiffel Tower when I will return to Paris.

4 Now until I'm 18 years old, I'm going to get a driver's license.

5 The decorating should be finished by the time the owner comes back.

D 주어진 문장과 같은 뜻이 되도록 빈칸을 채우시오.

1 Because Sam has moved to Austria, he can't see his friends often.

= _____ _____ Sam has moved to Austria, he can't see his friends often.

2 As soon as I saw my sister, I hugged her.

= _____ _____ I saw my sister, I hugged her.

= _____ seeing my sister, I hugged her.

WRITING PRACTICE

보기에 주어진 접속사를 이용하여 영작을 완성하시오.

보기	while	not/until	as soon as	after

1 내가 여행하는 동안, 나는 아주 좋은 사람들을 만났다.

_____ _____ _____ , I met such good people.

2 내가 그녀를 찾자마자 네게 전화를 걸겠다.

_____ _____ _____ _____ _____ ,

I'll call you.

3 나는 23살이 되어서야 해외여행을 했다.

I _____ _____ travel abroad _____ I was 23.

4 나는 저녁 식사를 한 후에 운동을 할 것이다.

I will work out _____ _____ _____ _____ .

☑ **CHECK UP**   괄호 안에서 알맞은 것을 고르시오.

1 You can get a free ticket (so that / only if) you're under 11.   `A-1`

2 Stay for dinner (unless / as long as) you're busy.   `A-1`

3 (Although / As) his writing shows, he will become a great author.   `C`

4 No matter (they say what / what they say), you are so beautiful.   `B`

5 (In case / Unless) you need to contact me, take your cellphone with you.   `A-3`

A   보기에서 가장 알맞은 접속사를 골라 빈칸에 쓰시오.

보기	in case	as long as	as	unless	although

1 _____ we all start helping each other, our team will never win.

2 You can borrow my book _____ you bring it back tomorrow.

3 I really enjoyed my trip to London _____ the weather was terrible.

4 You had better take the keys _____ I am late.

5 She passed her driving test, _____ I expected.

B   다음 a와 b의 문장을 바르게 연결하시오.

a	b

1 As yesterday was Sunday, •

2 You can come to the play •

3 She's going to stay home •

4 Although he has many qualifications, •

5 No matter how poorly you do, •

• a. he doesn't have a job.

• b. as long as you behave yourself.

• c. in case the electrician comes.

• d. you can always try again.

• e. I didn't have to go to school.

C 다음 문장에서 어법상 <u>틀린</u> 곳을 찾아 고치시오. 틀린 곳이 없으면 O표 하시오.

1 No matter how I often tell her, she doesn't listen.

2 Please call me if only you cannot attend.

3 I will prepare some extra food in case more people arrive.

4 It's such a nice day that we can enjoy surfing in the sea.

5 It was such cold that I wore a heavy coat.

D 다음 빈칸에 공통으로 들어갈 접속사를 쓰시오.

1 a. It became cold _____ the sun went down.

   b. The book is just _____ we expected from the author.

2 a. She didn't know _____ her mother was sick.

   b. The movie was so boring _____ I fell asleep.

   c. Save the file so _____ you can continue to work on it later.

3 a. I don't know _____ his story is true or not.

   b. Please contact customer service _____ the problem persists.

WRITING PRACTICE

보기에 주어진 접속사와 괄호 안의 말을 이용하여 영작을 완성하시오.

보기	even though	as	as long as	unless

1 내가 살아 있는 한 너를 절대 잊지 않을 거야. (live)

   I'll never forget you _____ _____ _____ _____.

2 그녀는 비록 최고의 점수를 받았지만 그 대학에 들어가지 않았다. (get the highest score)

   She didn't get into the university _____ _____ _____ _____
   _____ _____ _____.

3 그녀는 변호사로서 나와 함께 일한다. (lawyer)

   She works with me _____ _____ _____.

4 나는 잠잘 때가 아니면 항상 전화를 받는다. (be asleep)

   I always answer my phone _____ _____ _____ _____.

실전 TEST 03 Chapter 06-07

1 다음 중 밑줄 친 분사의 형태가 **틀린** 것을 고르시오.

① The actress was <u>welcomed</u> by her fans.
② He was <u>skiing</u> on the easiest slope.
③ It was an <u>excited</u> movie, wasn't it?
④ There were two candidates <u>running</u> for president.
⑤ I obtained information on accidents <u>occurring</u> at work.

2 다음 밑줄 친 부분의 쓰임이 **다른** 하나를 고르시오.

① You need to bring <u>dancing</u> shoes to tomorrow's dance class.
② I can't sleep well at night. I need to take a <u>sleeping</u> pill.
③ I saw some volunteers <u>planting</u> trees in the public park.
④ I'd like to try these on. Where is the <u>fitting</u> room?
⑤ Teens can open a <u>checking</u> account with a $5 deposit.

3 밑줄 친 부분이 어법상 **틀린** 것을 고르시오.

① It was very <u>exciting</u> to go camping with my father.
② The study's results are <u>interesting</u> in several respects.
③ You should figure out the <u>implying</u> meaning of the poem.
④ The benefits <u>offered</u> by a membership are remarkable.
⑤ This is the type of paper <u>used</u> for magazines.

4 괄호 안의 말을 알맞은 분사 형태로 바꾸시오.

(A) He read her message, _____ about how to answer it. (think)
(B) Before _____, switch off all the lights here. (leave)
(C) _____ how to deal with the problem, I wasn't worried. (know)
(D) _____ from work, I fell asleep. (tire)

5 우리말과 일치하도록 ⓐ, ⓑ에 알맞은 말을 쓰시오.

그 강의가 몹시 지루했기 때문에 많은 학생들은 거기에 집중하지 않았다.

→ The lecture was so _____ⓐ_____ that many students didn't pay _____ⓑ_____ to it.

6 밑줄 친 부분이 어법상 **틀린** 것을 고르시오.

My parents let me get my ear ① <u>piercing</u>. They kept ② <u>asking</u> if it was what I really wanted, but I finally persuaded them. The man at the shop started ③ <u>to count down</u> from three and pierced my ear on "two." It really ④ <u>didn't hurt</u> that much. I have to leave this earring in for six weeks and keep it very ⑤ <u>clean</u>.

7 다음 중 어법상 <u>틀린</u> 것을 고르시오.

① Having had no breakfast, I'm hungry now.
② Born into a rich family, he doesn't care about money.
③ Weather permitting, we'll go on a picnic tomorrow.
④ Famous for their beauty, diamonds are expensive.
⑤ Satisfying with the results, the research team decided to go ahead with the project.

8 빈칸에 알맞은 것을 고르시오.

_____ what I see in Korea, Korean youths are very smart.

① Judging from
② Assuming that
③ Frankly speaking
④ Generally speaking
⑤ Granted that

9 빈칸에 공통으로 들어갈 단어를 쓰시오.

(A) I'll welcome her _____ my arms wide open.
(B) _____ their baby sleeping in the next room, they watched TV.
(C) He is reading the newspaper _____ his legs crossed.

10 어법상 틀린 곳을 찾아 고치시오. (1개)

You embarrassed me! Considered that you are my best friend, your remarks were totally inappropriate. You even talked about me in front of strangers. I was deeply hurt by your actions.

[11-12] 빈칸에 공통으로 들어갈 접속사를 쓰시오.

11

(A) _____ I was away, everything changed.
(B) The first two services are free, _____ the third costs $10.

12

(A) I've earned a living _____ I was 15.
(B) I'm always on a diet, _____ I put on weight easily.

13 우리말과 일치하도록 괄호 안의 말을 활용하여 문장을 완성하시오.

여행을 하고 나서야 우리는 다른 문화를 이해할 수 있다. (not until, understand, cultures)

→ _____ _____ we travel _____ we _____ other _____.

14 다음 중 어법상 맞는 것을 고르시오.

① Let's go as soon as Debbie arrives.
② Not only my parents but my brother hate cats.
③ The pilot as well as flight attendants are wearing uniform.
④ Sightseeing is best done either by tour bus and by bicycles.
⑤ Professor Kim cannot speak neither English nor Spanish.

15 (A), (B) 각각에 들어갈 단어를 쓰시오.

(A) Lower the heat, _____ the soup will burn.
(B) Go to church right now, _____ you won't be late.

16 다음 중 어법상 틀린 것을 고르시오.

① What do you believe is true?
② She asked me if I was single.
③ Nobody knows what the answer is.
④ You must tell me what did he tell you.
⑤ Do you know how he escaped from prison?

17 빈칸에 공통으로 들어갈 단어를 쓰시오.

(A) I love movies. I hardly ever go to the movies with friends, _____.
(B) _____ she is rich and pretty, no one wants to be her friend.

18 [보기]의 as와 의미가 같은 것을 고르시오.

[보기] When in Rome, do as the Romans do.

① Another policeman was injured as fighting continued.
② I'll treat them as I'd like to be treated.
③ The news apparently came as a complete surprise.
④ Students barely read books, as they have so much homework to do.
⑤ As we got there, the concert began.

19 다음 중 밑줄 친 부분의 쓰임이 틀린 것을 고르시오.

① Let's check to see if there is a mistake.
② I liked your suggestion that we go to the beach.
③ It's a pity that we didn't meet sooner.
④ I was wondering that you could help me.
⑤ It doesn't matter whether he is rich or poor.

[20-21] 빈칸에 알맞은 것을 고르시오.

20
_____ much you love him, he does not love you.

① Unless   ② How
③ Even if   ④ As soon as
⑤ No matter how

21

_____ the party is over, the house is calm and empty.

① Only if   ② Now that
③ In case   ④ So that
⑤ Whereas

[22-24] 다음을 읽고, 물음에 답하시오.

I recently bought a special liquid to clear a (A) [blocking / blocked] pipe in my kitchen. I read the instructions carefully: "Pour 500 ml into the clogged pipe." 액체를 측정할 물건을 찾아 주위를 돌아보고 난 후, I could find only a 50 ml plastic cup. After carefully pouring the (B) [cleaning / cleaned] liquid into the cup, then into the pipe, exactly 10 times, I saw that the container was empty. Feeling somewhat (C) [cheating / cheated], I looked again at the instructions. At the bottom it read, "Contents: 500 ml."

22 (A), (B), (C)의 각 네모 안에서 어법에 맞는 표현을 골라 짝지은 것을 고르시오.

	(A)	(B)	(C)
①	blocking	cleaning	cheating
②	blocking	cleaned	cheated
③	blocked	cleaning	cheating
④	blocked	cleaning	cheated
⑤	blocked	cleaned	cheating

23 위 글의 밑줄 친 우리말과 일치하도록 괄호 안의 말을 활용하여 빈칸을 채우시오.

_____ _____ for something _____ _____ the liquid with
(look around, measure)

24 "I"의 심정으로 가장 알맞은 것을 고르시오.

① 허탈하다   ② 행복하다
③ 슬프다   ④ 부끄럽다
⑤ 질투가 난다

[25-26] 다음 글을 읽고, 물음에 답하시오.

Rain forests ① used to cover as much as 14% of the Earth's land. Today they cover less than 6%. In fact, rain forests are disappearing ② at a frightening speed: An area of rain forest as big as 20 football fields ③ is cut or burned down each minute. This means they will all be gone ④ by the time you grow up ⑤ unless we don't take action to save them.

25 ①~⑤ 중, 어법상 틀린 것을 고르시오.

①   ②   ③   ④   ⑤

26 rain forests에 대한 위 글의 내용과 일치하지 않는 것을 고르시오.

① 과거에 지구 육지 면적의 14%를 차지했다.
② 오늘날 지구 육지 면적의 6%도 차지하지 않는다.
③ 굉장히 빠른 속도로 사라지고 있다.
④ 매 시간 축구장 면적의 20배가 사라지고 있다.
⑤ 지금 노력하지 않으면 나중에는 모두 사라질 것이다.

최종 TEST 01

[1-3] 빈칸에 알맞은 것을 고르시오.

1

> The company's profits _____ since last year.

① increase   ② are increasing
③ increased   ④ have increased
⑤ will increase

2

> It can be difficult _____ children to understand emotions.

① by   ② of   ③ for
④ with   ⑤ to

3

> The Internet is useful for _____ large amount of information at once.

① find   ② to find
③ finding   ④ found
⑤ have found

[4-5] 우리말과 일치하도록 괄호 안의 말을 활용하여 문장을 완성하시오.

4

> 그녀는 조간 신문의 기사를 쓰느라 바빴다. (write)

→ She _____ _____ _____ an article for the morning paper.

5

> 중국어는 세계에서 가장 많은 사람들에 의해 말해진다. (speak)

→ Chinese _____ _____ _____ the most people in the world.

6 빈칸에 들어갈 수 <u>없는</u> 것을 고르시오.

> I _____ to communicate by email.

① want   ② would like
③ hope   ④ prefer
⑤ enjoy

[7-9] 우리말과 일치하도록 괄호 안의 말을 바르게 배열하시오.

7

> 선생님은 그가 지각한 것에 대해 아무 말도 하지 않았다.
> (say, about, didn't, anything, him, being, late)

→ The teacher _____

_____.

8

> 그는 잠들지 않기 위해 커피를 마셨다.
> (drank, so, coffee, fall, as, to, asleep, not)

→ He _____

_____.

9

그녀는 자기가 미행당하고 있다는 것을 몰랐다.
(followed, know, didn't, she, being, was, that)

→ She _____

_____ .

10 [보기]의 crying과 쓰임이 같은 것을 고르시오.

[보기]   Who is that crying girl?

① She woke up and heard the birds singing.
② The people standing in line became tired of waiting.
③ The boy came running into the room.
④ I was taking a shower when you called.
⑤ You should not keep her waiting.

[11-13] 두 문장이 같은 의미가 되도록 빈칸에 알맞은 말을 쓰시오.

11

My best friend made me this bracelet.
→ This bracelet _____ _____
_____ _____ by my best friend.

12

Jim was so scared that he couldn't go to bed.
→ Jim was too _____ _____
_____ _____ _____ .

13

You can't get in if you don't have a reservation.
→ You can't get in _____ you have _____ _____ .

[14-16] 우리말을 영어로 바르게 옮긴 것을 고르시오.

14

너는 네 증상에 대해 의사와 상담하는 것이 낫다.

① You might consult a doctor about your symptoms.
② You had better consult a doctor about your symptoms.
③ You should have consulted a doctor about your symptoms.
④ You are going to consult a doctor about your symptoms.
⑤ You will have to consult a doctor about your symptoms.

15

아버지가 집에 왔을 때 우리는 저녁 식사를 마친 후였다.

① We had finished dinner when my father came home.
② We finished dinner when my father had come home.
③ We finished dinner when my father came home.
④ We will have finished dinner when my father comes home.
⑤ We will finish dinner when my father comes home.

16

그는 고개를 기울인 채 나를 빤히 바라보았다.

① He stared at me tilting.
② He stared at me with his head tilt.
③ He stared at me with his head tilted.
④ He stared at me with his head tilting.
⑤ He stared at me his head tilted.

[17-18] 밑줄 친 부분 중 어법상 틀린 것을 골라 바르게 고치시오.

17

I think those three books recommending
___①___   ___②___
by my English teacher will definitely show
                              ___③___
you how you can improve your English
        ___④___
quickly.

18

I worked at this company since it started.
  ___①___   ___②___
I will have been working here for 10 years
        ___③___   ___④___
next year.

19 다음 중 어법상 <u>틀린</u> 것을 고르시오.

① I was lucky to have met you.
② He was ashamed of making a mistake.
③ Text me when you arrive at the station.
④ When asking about what happened, he refused to answer.
⑤ I forgot to turn off the stove, so the entire kitchen is filled with smoke.

20 [보기]의 <u>can</u>과 의미가 같은 것을 고르시오.

[보기] You <u>can</u> take photos as long as you don't use a flash.

① <u>Can</u> you play the guitar?
② I <u>can</u> speak French fluently.
③ Vitamins <u>can</u> help you relieve stress.
④ <u>Can</u> I park my car in front of the building?
⑤ <u>Can</u> this schedule be right? It seems too short.

21 빈칸에 공통으로 들어갈 말로 알맞은 것을 고르시오.

• We _____ respect each other's opinions.
• You _____ have bought the gift earlier.

① can   ② should
③ used to   ④ had better
⑤ would rather

Some people don't like eating hot peppers (A) [because / because of] the strong burning feeling it gives them. On the other hand, there are some birds that really love hot peppers! In fact, some hot peppers are such a major food source for certain birds ⓐ that they are called "bird peppers." These birds don't seem to have the same reaction that humans do when they eat them. This is because birds have far fewer *taste buds. (B) [Unless / If] birds don't eat hot peppers for their flavor, then why do they love them? Some researchers believe the spicy taste of hot peppers keeps other animals away, and this leaves them for the birds. By (C) [eating / eat] the peppers, birds spread the seeds of the plant ⓑ (in different areas, so that, grow, can, new peppers).

*taste bud (혀의) 미뢰

22 위 글의 ⓐ that과 쓰임이 같은 것을 고르시오.

① It is natural that he got angry.
② They liked the idea that the old building will be changed to a museum.
③ She was so embarrassed that she felt like crying.
④ I didn't know that he had released a new album.
⑤ He told me that I should forward the email to you.

23 위 글의 ⓑ를 문맥과 어법상 바르게 배열하시오.

24 (A), (B), (C) 각 네모 안에서 어법에 맞는 표현을 골라 짝지은 것을 고르시오.

	(A)		(B)		(C)
①	because	······	Unless	······	eating
②	because of	······	If	······	eating
③	because	······	If	······	eating
④	because of	······	Unless	······	eat
⑤	because	······	If	······	eat

You may not think spiders and grasshoppers look tasty, but ⓐ it is believed that more than 80 percent of the people in the world eat bugs. For example, in Thailand, fried scorpions on a stick ① eat as a snack. And in Mexico, some people enjoy ② toasted grasshoppers. Interestingly, bugs are actually healthy because they're high in protein and low in fat. In addition, some scientists think ③ that they may offer a solution to the world's food problem. This is because they are much easier and cheaper ④ to raise than common animal food sources, such as pigs and cows. Also, more than 3,600 types of bugs are safe to eat. So there are many tasty bugs ⑤ to choose from!

25 위 글의 ⓐ와 같은 의미가 되도록 빈칸에 알맞은 말을 쓰시오.

→ More than _____
are _____.

26 ①~⑤ 중에서 어법상 틀린 것을 고르시오.

①   ②   ③   ④   ⑤

최종 TEST 02

[1-2] 빈칸에 알맞은 것을 고르시오.

1

Steve _____ for the company for five years.

① work   ② works
③ working   ④ been working
⑤ has worked

2

Their classroom was filled _____ colorful balloons for the party.

① at   ② by
③ with   ④ over
⑤ of

3   빈칸에 들어갈 말로 알맞은 것으로 짝지은 것을 고르시오.

- It was nice _____ you to forgive him.
- It would be difficult _____ children to understand this article.

① by – for   ② for - by
③ to - of   ④ of - for
⑤ for - of

4   다음 문장을 수동태로 바꾸어 쓰시오.

> The teacher told the students to stay after class.
>
> → _____

[5-6] 다음 대화의 빈칸에 알맞은 말을 고르시오.

5

A: Must I bring my own computer?
B: No, _____.

① you must
② you don't have to
③ you cannot
④ you must not
⑤ you shouldn't have

6

A: When _____ on the business trip?
B: Early next month.

① are you going
② did you go
③ may you go
④ have you gone
⑤ have you been going

7   우리말과 일치하도록 괄호 안의 말을 활용하여 문장을 완성하시오.

> 당신은 다른 이들을 방해하지 않는 한 노트북을 사용해도 됩니다. (as long as, disturb)

→ You may use your laptop _____

_____.

8 [보기]의 that과 쓰임이 같은 것을 고르시오.

> [보기] Is it true <u>that</u> he was accepted to law school?

① I had no evidence <u>that</u> Jack was a thief.
② Did you know <u>that</u> Mike quit his job?
③ I think <u>that</u> you should apologize to her.
④ It is well known <u>that</u> exercise helps you feel better.
⑤ His mistake was <u>that</u> he didn't report the incident to his boss.

[9-10] 우리말을 영어로 바르게 옮긴 것을 고르시오.

9
> 당신은 그가 나가도록 허락하지 말았어야 했다.

① You should allow him go out.
② You should allow him to go out.
③ You must not have allowed him go out.
④ You cannot have allowed him to go out.
⑤ You shouldn't have allowed him to go out.

10
> 내가 일본을 다시 방문할 때 이곳에서 머무르길 바란다.

① I hope staying here when I visit Japan again.
② I hope to stay here when I visit Japan again.
③ I hope staying here when visiting Japan again.
④ I hope to stay here when I will visit Japan again.
⑤ I hope that I will stay here when I will visit Japan again.

[11-12] 두 문장이 같은 의미가 되도록 빈칸에 알맞은 말을 쓰시오.

11
> It is foolish to believe in superstitions.
> → _____ _____ _____ is foolish.

12
> It is said that potatoes were introduced to Europe in the 1500s.
> → Potatoes _____ _____ _____ _____ _____ to Europe in the 1500s.

[13-14] 다음 중 어법상 틀린 것을 고르시오.

13 ① Do you know the man staring at us?
② A new school is being built in the city.
③ Used carefully, it will prove quite helpful.
④ My parents wanted me to stay with them.
⑤ I have seen the movie when it was released.

14 ① For exercise, I prefer running to cycling.
② She had to stop swimming because of shoulder problems.
③ I suggested that she looks for another job.
④ He watched the suspect get out of the car.
⑤ We were talking about whether the car was worth buying.

15

> Had nothing else to do, I started reading the book.

16

> Avoid to eat too much if you want to stay fit.

17 주어진 문장과 같은 의미가 되도록 빈칸을 완성하시오.

> (A) It seems that Sara has no friends.
>   → Sara _____.
> (B) That we won the match surprised everyone.
>   → It _____.

18 [보기]의 would와 의미가 같은 것을 고르시오.

> [보기] When he was a child, he would play with his brother in the playground.

① Would you like some tea?
② Mary said she would call me.
③ They wouldn't change their mind.
④ We would go on picnics in the summer.
⑤ I would appreciate it if you could send me the file.

19 빈칸에 들어갈 수 없는 것을 고르시오.

> A : What is Jake doing?
> B : He _____ be working out at the gym.

① may
② might
③ could
④ is able to
⑤ must

20 빈칸에 알맞은 것을 모두 고르시오.

> A : Your car really needs _____.
> B : Yeah, I should have done it yesterday.

① wash
② washed
③ to wash
④ washing
⑤ to be washed

21 다음 대화문에서 밑줄 친 부분이 어색한 것을 고르시오.

① A : He is such a hard worker.
   B : Yes. I'm thinking he will succeed.
② A : What did you do last weekend?
   B : I went shopping with my mother.
③ A : Have you ever taken his class?
   B : Yes, but it was really boring.
④ A : How are you feeling today?
   B : Not very good.
⑤ A : Sue seems sick today.
   B : She left her lunch untouched.

Will your child grow up ⓐ to become a successful athlete? You might not have to wait to find out. Scientists believe ① that they have discovered the gene that makes people good at sports. To test a person's genes, researchers examine cells ② taking from the inside of his or her mouth. They then look for a specific gene that produces a protein known as ACTN3. Our muscles use this protein ③ when they need extra energy. For this reason, it helps people ④ become better athletes. There are two types of ACTN3. The first, known as R, is good for ⑤ moving very quickly for short periods of time. The second, known as X, is more useful for sports that require moving long distances, such as marathons.

22 위 글의 ⓐ to become과 쓰임이 같은 것을 고르시오.

① Jamie left home in order to get a job.
② I need something to read on my flight.
③ I'm so sad to hear about your loss.
④ I'd like to speak to your manager.
⑤ He woke up to find himself alone in the room.

23 ①~⑤ 중에서 어법상 틀린 것을 고르시오.

① ② ③ ④ ⑤

Paris has a huge, complex sewer system. It pumps around 75 billion gallons of wastewater each year. But it might also be one of the city's greatest unused sources of energy. And more importantly, the energy that comes from it won't run out. Now, engineers and city planners hope to use this energy (A) to heat / heating a school. The sewers collect lots of warm wastewater from baths, showers, dishwashers, and kitchen sinks every day. _____ⓐ_____, the water in the sewers can be as hot as 20 degrees Celsius. Engineers plan to run a special fluid through a pipe. It will collect heat and then flow into the school's basement, where a machine will pump it throughout the school. This project (B) expects / is expected to meet 70 percent of the school's heating needs. (C) If / Because the project works well, then other buildings will receive the same treatment—even the Presidential Palace!

24 (A), (B), (C)의 각 네모 안에서 어법에 맞는 표현을 골라 짝지은 것을 고르시오.

	(A)	(B)	(C)
①	to heat	expects	If
②	heating	expects	If
③	to heat	is expected	If
④	heating	is expected	Because
⑤	to heat	is expected	Because

25 빈칸 ⓐ에 들어갈 말로 알맞은 것을 고르시오.

① As a result ② Similarly
③ However ④ On the other hand
⑤ Moreover

지은이

NE능률 영어교육연구소

NE능률 영어교육연구소는 혁신적이며 효율적인 영어 교재를 개발하고
영어 학습의 질을 한 단계 높이고자 노력하는 NE능률의 연구조직입니다.

GRAMMAR ZONE WORKBOOK 〈기본편 1〉

펴 낸 이	주민홍
펴 낸 곳	서울특별시 마포구 월드컵북로 396(상암동) 누리꿈스퀘어 비즈니스타워 10층 (주)NE능률 (우편번호 03925)
펴 낸 날	2017년 1월 5일 개정판 제1쇄 2024년 1월 15일 제18쇄
전　　화	02 2014 7114
팩　　스	02 3142 0356
홈페이지	www.neungyule.com
등록번호	제 1-68호
I S B N	979-11-253-1237-6　53740
정　　가	6,500원

NE 능률

고객센터

교재 내용 문의 : contact.nebooks.co.kr (별도의 가입 절차 없이 작성 가능)
제품 구매, 교환, 불량, 반품 문의 : 02-2014-7114
☎ 전화문의는 본사 업무시간 중에만 가능합니다.

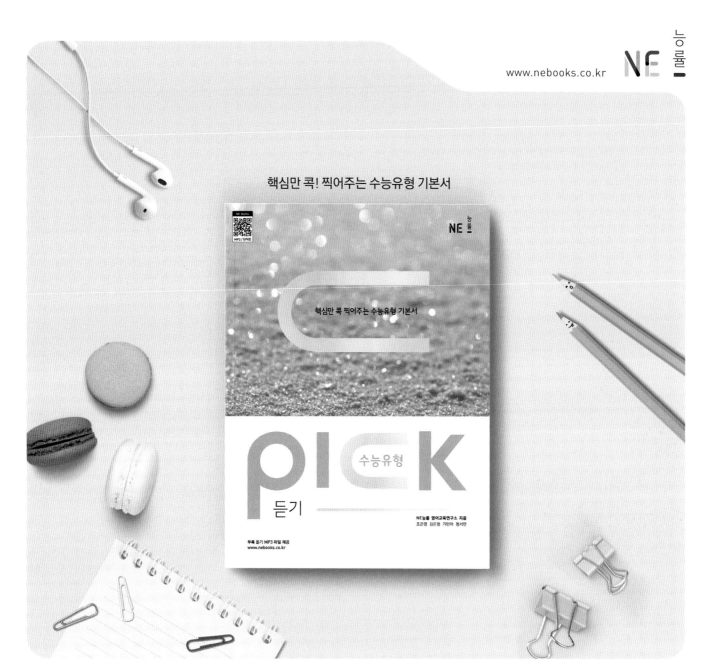

The Standard for English Grammar Books

GRAMMAR ZONE
WORKBOOK

ZONE

기본편 1

www.nebooks.co.kr

NE능률 영어교육연구소
한정은 배연희 이하나 송민아

NE 능률

영수

NE능률이
영어도, 수학도 **잘합니다.**

창의사고력은 풍부하게, 개념 확립은 탄탄하게,
수학으로 만나는 NE능률의 1등 노하우!
배움은 즐거워지고 자신감은 커져갑니다.

1등 영어브랜드로 지켜온 믿음, 변함없이 수학교육으로 이어가겠습니다.

초등 개념기본서

초등 상위권 심화학습서

초등고학년 최상위 개념서

중등 개념기본서

중등 유형기본서

중등 상위권 심화학습서

고등 단기학습공략서

건강한
배움의 즐거움